# Civil War Voices
## from
## Western North Carolina

## Letters from the Battlefield
## and the Home Front

Louisa Emmons

ISBN-13: 978-0692468333 (Hollow Tree Press)
ISBN-10: 0692468331

Hollow Tree Press
P.O. Box 322
Morganton, NC 28680

Cover image: Meeting of General William Sherman and General Joseph Johnston on the Hillsboro Road prior to Johnston's surrender on April 26, 1865.

To Joe Alexander
who knew Civil War history better than anyone

# CONTENTS

"The enduring realization is that when a great challenge comes, the most ordinary people can show that they value something more than they value their own lives."

- Bruce Catton

# PREFACE

When I decided to write this book, I was prepared to search through a large number of Civil War letters. What I hoped to find was some kind of unifying theme among them that would tie my book together. Without knowing what that would be, I suspected it might have something to do with a shared animosity toward the United States government and a powerful determination to win the war. There were certainly elements of this theme running through the letters, but in no way did I find this to be a dominant theme. What I did discover, to my surprise, were overwhelming expressions of love for family and homeland. In fact, I was not prepared for the depth of feeling that poured out of the letters from soldiers and family members. The contents of these letters are deeply personal and moving: grief over the loss of a child; a desperate longing to return to mountain homes; gnawing hunger; the hard lives of women left alone to raise children and tend farms; the misery of soldiers constantly subjected to harsh weather and fierce battles; and sometimes warmth and humor even during the most difficult times. I was touched by the courage and the strength of so many of my fellow North Carolinians. More than once, I thought how proud I was of them. And I thought, too, that I wanted my book to be a tribute to them.

The letters featured in this book were taken largely from family collections of Civil War letters housed in academic institutions of North Carolina. These are the letters that have been passed down for generations and generously donated to universities for the purpose of disseminating information about Civil War life to the public. Some of the letters are still privately owned by families. Every effort has been made to retain the original spelling and, wherever possible, the original layout of the letters. As a whole, these letters represent the diversity of social class and political philosophy in western North Carolina during the Civil War. And yet, they are far more than that. These letters express the deepest longings of loved ones separated by war. As you read them I hope you will remember that you and I are the uninvited guests gazing through a narrow window into lives that, once so animated by hope and sorrow, are now only a memory.

# 1. WESTERN NORTH CAROLINA
# IN THE CIVIL WAR

The long-accepted view of western North Carolina in the Civil War as a monolithic society with a shared cultural, political and social philosophy is flawed. Far from being united, three distinct groups comprised the sociopolitical landscape of western North Carolina in the Civil War: the unaffiliated citizen who wished to live in peace without taking sides, the loyal confederate who fought for southern independence, and the southern Unionist who maintained allegiance to the federal government. Personal loyalties were sometimes difficult to define and were interpreted from family to family. Many wished to remain neutral, some felt unsafe revealing their allegiance for fear of reprisal, some were adamant in the defense of their beliefs. It was a time filled with turbulence, anger and suspicion. It was an uneasy co-existence which could erupt into bitter and violent internecine warfare. Sometimes it led to disastrous confrontations as in the case of the Shelton Laurel Massacre in Madison County in 1863. Clearly, the story of western North Carolina during the Civil War is a study in contrasts between the privileged and the poor, the obedient soldier and the deserter, the Confederate and the Unionist.

Though fewer in number than in the coastal plains counties of the state, the western counties had their share of the wealthy planter class with slaves, vast acreages and business transactions which helped to provide employment and structure to its mountain towns. The leaders of the Confederate cause were largely drawn from this class which was more educated and wealthier than the vast ranks of the mountaineer infantry they commanded. The planter class fought for a way of life which had brought them privilege and respect.

A large number of mountain people felt no particular allegiance philosophically to either the North or the South. They wished to live their lives, raise their families and grow their crops without interference from the government. Suspicion was felt toward the ruling white class whose goals had little in common with the poor, uneducated mountain farmer. Maintaining a system of slave labor which was vital to the existence of the planter class had little meaning for mountaineers.

Southern Unionists, referred to as "Tories" in western North Carolina as a measure of the distaste in which they were held by many, existed in numbers that remain difficult to determine. Widely varying estimates of individuals maintaining at least a philosophical loyalty to the union exist. Entire families were Unionists in some cases, but there were also families which were divided in their allegiances. It is clear, however, that these southern Unionists existed in far greater numbers in the mountains of western North Carolina than elsewhere in the state. They sometimes found their way to join the philosophically similar and geographically neighboring eastern armies of Tennessee which were decidedly in favor of the union and fought with it. Eastern Tennessee was clearly the hub of union activity in that state. In fact, the East Tennessee Convention met and voted on three different occasions during the Civil War to attempt secession from Tennessee in order to form a pro-Union state within Tennessee. For North Carolina Unionists, it was a dangerous proposition to ally oneself with the acknowledged enemy; being a southern Unionist in a confederate state was a difficult philosophical position to justify.

Conscripting mountain soldiers into the Confederate army presented its own problems, particularly to a unique region of North Carolina cut off from the state's mainstreams of commerce, banking and educational opportunity. It represented intrusive and troubling governmental interference to men who felt little allegiance to the southern cause. Many citizens of the western counties suspected and resented that the Civil War in the south was being waged largely to maintain the lifestyle of the ruling class. As a result, western North Carolina experienced large numbers of deserters during the Civil War, some of whom enlisted with Union forces after deserting the ranks of the Confederate army. These deserters often hid out in the woods to avoid capture, sometimes banding together with fellow deserters and Unionists, and skirmishing with Confederate authorities. Toward the end of the war in particular, the farmers of the western counties began to question why they were enduring starvation and misery, long rain-soaked marches in worn boots and dry dusty summers sleeping on the parched ground as they watched friends and comrades suffer horrific deaths day in and day out. Many felt the call to return home to plant the poor and rocky fields which provided food for the families they left behind, and some chose to remain there rather than return to the call of duty.

It should be noted that North Carolina, in general, was not disposed favorably toward secession from the Union, being the last of the southern states to secede. Fiery debate and four separate votes on separate occasions were required to draw North Carolina into the Confederacy. Many felt reluctant to dissolve the union which had been so hard-fought for and won by their grandfathers, and many foresaw bitter days ahead for a state with an agrarian economy and little industrial activity to produce the machinery of war. The final break came with President Lincoln's order to fire upon Fort Sumter and his call for federal troops to quell the unrest in South Carolina. This was the unwitting action that unintentionally united the confederate states. Following the Battle of Fort Sumter, on May 20, 1861, North Carolina joined the Confederacy.

# 2. BUNCOMBE COUNTY COLLECTIONS

## Clayton Family Papers, 1855-1922

Thomas Clayton (1934-1905) served as a military storekeeper at the Confederate Armory on College Street in Asheville, NC. He entered the Civil War late, in 1864, and reported for duty in Columbia, SC., where he served for one month before being assigned to an engineering unit in General Hood's Corps. Clayton was stationed in Georgia during the Atlanta campaign, and was later a member of General Stephen Lee's Corps in Alabama. Thomas Clayton married Emma Adelaide Smith (1839-1922) who remained in Asheville for the duration of the war with their children. After the war, Clayton became a contractor for the Western Railroad in North Carolina.

Thomas Clayton's father, Colonel Ephraim Clayton, owned a factory in Asheville which produced Enfield-style rifles initially rejected for use by the Confederacy. When the Confederate government took over the company in 1862, superior weapons began to be produced under the direction of Major Benjamin Sloan. Iron mines near Tennessee provided the raw products used in the manufacture of the guns, and by early 1863 the company produced 300 rifles per month. The Armory was destroyed in 1865 when the Union army entered Asheville.

## Roland C. Osborne and Keziah Stradley Osborne Civil War Papers

Roland Calloway Osborne was (probably) born in 1837. He enlisted on June 29, 1861 in Haywood County. The companies which were to form the 25th NC Regiment in which Osborne served began to organize in western North Carolina in May 1861 and to assemble at Camp Patton in Asheville. Company F was commanded by Capt. Thomas I. Lenoir, and then Capt. James M. Cathey who was killed at the Crater in Petersburg in 1864, then finally Capt. James A. Blaylock. Roland Osborne died July 3, 1863 at Petersburg, Virginia. He was married to Keziah Hasseltine Stradley (1838-1908), daughter of Thomas Stradley and Mary Frances Dibley.

# Zebulon Baird Vance-Harriett N. Espy Vance Letters
## and Zebulon Baird Vance (1824-1915) Papers

Governor Zebulon Baird Vance was a native of Buncombe County, North Carolina. Portions of two collections of his letters and papers have been included here. Of particular interest are the personal letters between Vance and his wife Hattie which reveal a gentle and loving family man so much in contrast to the outspoken and fiery politician. Here,Vance seems to find relief from the frantic world of politics by drawing close to those who are dearest to him. The other collection, the Zebulon Baird Vance (1824-1915) Papers are comprised chiefly of political correspondence.

Zebulon Baird Vance (1830-1894) was born in Buncombe County, North Carolina. He attended local schools and enrolled at thirteen in Washington College in eastern Tennessee. Vance read law in 1850 under John W. Woodfin of Asheville and thereafter attended the University of North Carolina to continue his legal studies. He was licensed to practice law in 1852, returned to Asheville, and was quickly elected solicitor for Buncombe County. In 1853 he was admitted to practice in the superior courts.

Vance entered North Carolina politics as a Whig but later aligned himself with the American or "Know-Nothing Party." In 1858, after serving one term in the North Carolina House of Commons (later the House of Representatives), he was elected to the 35th Congress. He also won a seat in the 36th Congress (1859-61) which was the last Congress before the South seceded from the Union.

Vance was opposed to secession, believing the Union should remain intact, but his views changed when Fort Sumter was fired upon and President Lincoln called up troops to settle the unrest in South Carolina.

Vance served as the commander of the "Rough and Ready Guards" beginning in May 1861. The "Guards" became Company F, 14th NC Regiment, serving in Virginia. In August 1861 Vance was elected colonel of the 26th North Carolina Regiment, which he commanded at New Bern in March 1862 and again in the Seven Days fighting before Richmond.

Vance accepted the Conservative party nomination for governor in 1862 and defeated railroad executive William Johnston of Mecklenburg County because of a genera dissatisfaction with the state's leadership and because of the uncertainties of war.

As war governor Vance worked tirelessly to provide for North Carolina troops and civilians, often clashing bitterly with President Jefferson Davis when it seemed the best interests of North Carolina citizens were compromised. When he received the news that General Johnston had surrendered his forces to Sherman on April 26, 1865 in Durham, Vance issued his final proclamation to the people of North Carolina before surrendering himself to Union General John Schofield. He was released but later arrested on May 13, 1865 at his home in Statesville on his thirty-fifth birthday. He was sent to Washington, D.C. and placed in the Old Capitol Prison for two months, but no charge was ever brought against him.

Vance filed an application for pardon from President Andrew Johnson on May 29, 1865. It was granted on 11 Mar. 1867. He returned to North Carolina and formed a law partnership in Charlotte and was elected to the U.S. Senate in 1870, but could not take his seat because of his former affiliation with the Confederacy. After a bitter campaign, Vance was elected to a third term of office as governor of North Carolina at the end of Reconstruction. Vance served his third term as governor for only two years before being elected to the United States Senate. He held his seat until his death.

Zebulon Vance died in 1894 at his home in Washington and was buried in Asheville. His first wife was Harriett Espy of Quaker Meadows, Burke County. They had four sons: Robert Espy, Charles Noel, David Mitchell, and Zebulon Baird, Jr.. Harriet Vance died in 1878. In 1880 Vance married a widow, Florence Steele Martin of Louisville, Ky., who survived him. They had no children.

## C. C. McPhail to Thomas Clayton[1]

Columbia, S.C.
Dec. 19th 1863.
Mr. Thos. Clayton
Mr. S. K. & [in?] Chg Armory,

Sir,

Your last letter, I havnt it by me & cannot refer to date, advises me of the sending off another train of wagons. If there is any danger of a big raid you must make every exertion to get every thing away at once, I wish that you were able to have wagons enough to bring off the whole affair. I was under the impression that one of the Pattons wished to hire his teams.

No chairs, desks, or stairs etc. can be had here. Bring on all the office furniture als that larger press which stood in the store room. Great complaints from many sources reach me about your sale of iron etc. I believe that you have discharged the trust I reposed in you with fidelity & to the best of your ability. I make it ever a point to sustain my officers as long as I find them worthy of my confidence.

When you leave I wish that you would request Capt Bailey to assume charge of the Armory Building etc. Have the guard to report to him.

Tell Mr. Kitzmiller that I wish to know when he is coming on. I don't wish him to remain longer than there is good reason for him to do so.

I don't know that I have any more instructions to give than you have already received. Hurry up

Very Respectfully, etc.
C. C. McPhail Capt
Comdg Armory

C. C. McPhail
Comdg C. S. Armory
Columbia S.C.
Dec 19th 1863

## Emma Clayton to Thomas Clayton[2]

Sunday Eve, April 24th [1864]

My own dear absent Husband,

You can not imagine how very sad and lonely I have been all day. I do think I never saw it rain more constantly than it has all morning and this evening there is strong indications of a thunder storm.

I feel this evening that I would give the world (were it mine to give) if I could only be with you. I never felt so sad as I do, it seems to me that I can see nothing but a long and weary life before me, for I can see no end to this war. Were the Yankees to make a peace (satisfactory to us) tomorrow, I would have no confidence in it for I believe from what I read in the papers, that they are becoming more enraged every day, at their own condition, and I do not believe they will ever allow us to live in peace again, for they are certainly a ruined people.

But now I know you are ready to say, hush Emma, you must not look on the dark side of the picture. Well my dear I know all that, but I can't help it, I've tried to be cheerful since you left and I think I have done very well so far, but as the days pass by, I realize more fully my lonely condition, and the great responsibility that is resting upon me, and indeed I don't think it at all strange, that I should have the blues. You must try and bear with me, perhaps I will feel better after a while.

Well well the sun is shining out again, we have just had a very hard shower, this is more like real old fashioned April weather than any thing we have had this spring. We have had some very pleasant weather since you left home. The children do enjoy it so much. Ephie says she loves the warm weather, because he loves God. He is a good boy I have nothing to complain of. But Ann is a hard child to govern. I have a great deal of trouble with her.

O! my dear one, how I wish I could see you this evening. If I could only look in upon you (wherever you are) I could cheer up and not have the blues again tonight. I wonder where you are and what you are doing? I hope you are at your journey's end and safe and sound and I know what you are doing – thinking of the dear ones at home. O! when shall we all meet again? Perhaps we may never meet again in this world. But there is a brighter home my dear husband, where there is no war nor bloodshed and where parting is not know where I hope we will an unbroken family be permitted to meet never to part again. O! what a consolation it is to me, to think that our Heavenly Father has prepared such a home for us, and given us the means by which we may reach that blissful place.

O! that He may help us to live with eternity in view for "we know not the day nor the hour when the son of men cometh."

Kate is not at home, she went with [Joe?] Ray to visit Alice Burnet. Ma, Pa, & all send much love to you. I do hope to get a long letter from you soon for I think it would do me so much good. Do write as often as you can, for it is my greatest pleasure now to read and answer your dear letters. Here anxiously I will sit and wait for the mails. Mother & Father are well. Remember me to cousin Thad, I hope you will get to be with or near him for he will be so much comfort for you. The children all send their dear Father many long sweet kisses. Good by my one dear husband. God bless and protect you is the prayer of your true and devoted wife.

Emma

## Thomas Clayton to Emma Clayton[3]

Head 2nd Lee's Corp
Near Palmetto, GA Sept 22nd, 1864

My Dear Emma,

Since writing you this on West Point and Atlanta RR, ? Nash Hardy has got a leave of absence for sixty days and goes home this evening. I have included to draft you a few lines by time Thursday it will reach you earlier than by the mail. I am very tired though and have but little more to write in the way of news than I had this morning. The indication today is that we will cross the River. In fact we have orders just received from Mjr Hd 2n to recommend the crossing of the River and I guess Hood will have us all in the saddle tonight and I dread it for it is now raining and will be very dark. But such is a soldier's life if he does his duty and I will try and do mine. But some of our Buncombe friends do not ? much about this but I spec he don't care. There is great dissatisfaction in his Regiment at his going away, and I expect many of the officers to resign or try to do so. The weather has been very bad for several days. Rain all the time and very dark my eyes are nearly out from hard use in making maps in such dark weather. It is now so dark I can hardly see where I am writing. If we should cross the River you must not looks for many letters from me. I will have little time to write and no way of sending my letters when written so you must not be weary about me if you do not hear from me often. I hope the campaign will soon end for this year. Then I will get to go home. I don't want to go before then, and Thomas and Col Preston have both promised me that I might go home. I have never asked for a leave nor I never will as long as I am needed here. I received your letter of the 12th. Ed Berry had not heard of Joe's marriage until today I told him. It was the first time I have seen him since we commenced to war. I think his opinions of ? is about like yours.

Thomas sends his love says tell them all he would write by Nash but has not time did not know he was going write this minute and has just come in from the line. Nash will start in a few minutes. I will close you my love to all at home so take good care of the children, God help them I wish I could see them. Farewell my dear and may the Father of mercy watch and protect you and then in the ? ? of you.

Devoted husband,
T. C.

Geo West is with me now don't forget to make the gloves for him. I feel under many obligations to him and he is a very clever man.

## Keziah Stradley Osborne to Roland C. Osborne[4]

January 1, 1862

1862 Beaverdam New year's day

A New Years gift, My Dear. Well what shall it be. I would love to give you a new years kiss this bright morning, but I won't so I will write you the very best letter that I can and send you my best wishes that this new year may be the happiest one of your life or least happier than the one just past May its closing day find you in your own quiet home surrounded by your dearest friends. May you be an orderly member of Christ's Church and an honorable citizen of an Independent Southern Confederacy May happiness dwell in your house and peace in reign in your Country. If it is the will of God that you remain here, if it is not May your happy Spirit be at rest in our Father's House, where there are many Mansions; in the New year's prayer of your absent Wife. After waiting longer than I ever have had to do before for a letter from you I received two last night. I found that you have been disappointed too. I suppose there has been something wrong about the mails. And right here I promise you that I will always do the very best I can about writing. You must remember that I can't always send to the Office at the right time. But be sure that I will not neglect to write on account of any thing being the matter. For if I can't write myself I will get some one else to do it. You ask me to help you fix a plan to get a [crop started; substitute ?] I think it very important for it to be done and if I was stout again like I used to be and was back in our house and could get good hands to work and the ground to work and the tools to work with and some clever girl to stay with me I would try to have thing ready for you. You know I always told you that I could beat you farming any how but you see there are a good many ands and ifs in the way. I can not walk yet and I am afraid I will not walk this winter. Dr. Neil now [?] thinks I can not walk in c [?] 12 months but I hope to get well sooner than that. I think your Father has rented nearly all his land and your farming tools are scattered to the four winds. Uncle Joseph is not ready to leave the house yet and you know that I could not do any good unless I could get to myself you know your Father would not care for any thing I could say. I still hope that you will get off to see to these things your self and I will then do what ever your interest requires if it is in my power to do so you had better believe I would love to be trying to make something for the children I got a letter from Sis Line [?] last night they are well and have sent you some butter cakes and apples. I hope you have got them. I will write to them about your pants. Addie promised to have them done by Christmas. I have a poor chance to work but I will do any thing I can for you. Fine [?] says she wants me to take the baby back and Mattie [?] says if Fine [?] wants a baby she may have one of her own for she can't share this big fat baby you [?] [she has had ?] so much trouble with him he is quite well this morning you ask me what a certain Lady means by signing her name so loving. I reckon she means what she says. If she does marry she will give a certain C.R. a most awful waking up. I think he has been dreaming this long time. By the way have you written C.R. [C.B.?] if you have not I wish you would. I know it would go against your feelings to do so but you know we must forgive if we hope to be forgiven and he has been very kind to me since you left. I would not care if he knowed some things I hate to see him made a fool of but I guess he will find out some day. I am so glad that you have got to house keeping. Do up you [?] it any better than you did last winter, or would you as soon be back on the hill with the same old housekeeper. We would have a nice piece of furniture now I mean a cradle. Jo [?] is at home yet his health is very delicate. I am afraid he can't stand the winter. His Col. don't take one bit of care of his men. They give him a dreadful mean name they have been ordered to Kentucky but the men have been starved and dragged about until they are unable to go. Don't be afraid of writing too much just wait till I grumble [?] I am much obliged to Billy Banham [Bonham ?] for his Kind wishes. I have often thought of him, that he would Be kind to you if you were sick. I have to hear how Any of the boys are doing you see I have filled up my Paper this time. I have just kissed Rufus for Papa he Is so sweet [?] I do want you to come and see him and kiss.

## Keziah Stradley Osborne to Roland C. Osborne[5]

I would be glad you could send me some postage stamp There is none at Asheville. It is so hard to get change

Beaverdam January 12th 1862

My Dear Husband

If you will stop over today I will give you a good dinner as this is my birthday. I am 24 years old today. I don't feel that old though I have been a widow for the past six months and sick one half the time and a cripple the other half besides missing this great big boy lying here in the cradle. Well – doubtless the largest half of my life is gone. I have no idea of living 24 years longer and what have I done! How much better is the world for my having lived in it for 24 years, very little if any. Perhaps one pathway has been brighter for my having walked a little way in it. Perhaps one heart is glad this morning that I have lived as long and have done. If so I have not lived entirely in vain, though I have often thought that I was a great deal more trouble to my friends than advantage to them yet I know they have assisted me cheerfully and this morning I am thankful that I have so many friends and I am right glad that I have a kind husband and a sweet little boy and that I am still able to do something for them. And oh how thankful I shall be that I have a Friend that sticketh closer than a Brother; One who has watched over me all my life and what has been with all my weakness and sin; and who has blessed me this morning again with every blessing that I need. Yet What have I done for him who died To save my soul from Death Nothing at all on the contrary I have received his spirit in ten thousand instances and if ever I am saved it will be by grace alone not for anything that I have done My Dear your letter of the 29th instant has reached me at last. You said you only started to write a page or two and I believe you wrote the best letter you ever did write. I must compliment you upon the improvement you have made in writing. I never saw any one improve so fast I am getting almost ashamed to send you my scribbling. I have written every letter that I ever have sent you on my lap while rocking the cradle and you know that is a poor way to write. However I am willing for you to beat me if you will only write often enough. I do love to read your kind loving letters. You stated that you had been doing something that you knew would grieve me and asked me to guess before I read what it was. But my curiosity was so great to see what it was that I could not wait to guess but read right on if I had guessed I would not have guess right for you know that card playing was one of two things that you promised me you would never do. I do not remind you of this to reproach you Dearest but to show you that I had confidence in you and I still have confidence in you. I believe you are trying to do right. I know it is hard to do right where you are, but God is able to help you and he will do it if you ask Him in the right way. It would have been distressing to me to have heard that you was indulging in card playing. I think it almost an altogether as great a sin as the use of Ardent Sprits, but on that point you and I always differed and I must touch it lightly. I suppose that many indulge in such sins for the want of something else to do. It would be a fine thing if there could be good reading matter sent to all the camps it would employ there leisure hours and keep them out of mischief. I got Joshua to write to Graves to send you the Tennessee Baptist. It has all the war news in it and a great deal of other good reading. Joshua says he wishes you would renew your subscription. You will see on the paper when your time will be out. I would send you the Asheville News but it is only half a sheet now, hardly worth the trouble let me know when you get the paper. Let me know if you have got the clothes you wanted. I feel bad because I could not find [fin ?] them for you myself. I have knit you a great big comfort. It is as nice as if it had been made at the North. Just poke your head over and I will wrap it round your neck. But I guess you don't need it bad to day. We don't need a fire here. I never saw such a winter before. We have had no cold weather worth speaking of. I am afraid it will be sickly where you are if it stays so warm. I see in the papers that there has been a little fight near Port Royall. I was glad to see that Clingman's Reg was not engaged. I always look for that I shall be glad if you get off without fighting if it could be possible, unless you could fight without being hurt yourselves. May be the warm weather will kill all the Yankees at the South. It is said there is 20,000 of them sick at Louisville, Kentucky. We have got a letter from Jo [?] since he returned to camp. His health is still bad. The Reg are nearly all sick. They are stationed on the Rail Road to guard it from Greenville to Chattanooga if you want to write to him you can direct to Strawberry Plains Tennessee, care of 29th Reg N.C. Volunteers, care Of Captain J. H. [?] Roberson [?]. I know he would be glad to hear from you. I got a letter from Sallie last week. She asked me to tell you that if you needed anything that they could help you to if you would let them know. They would be glad to help you. She says paper is getting so scarce there. She can't write much. Have you got enough to do you must [?] keep enough to write to me on. I have got a pretty good supply laid by. I think you must have missed getting a letter that I wrote about the time I thought you was coming home. I mentioned something that I wanted you to bring me in it. You missed the best letter that I ever wrote you when you left Wilmington. I have not told You any thing about your boy yet. He is well to day but he has a good many little sick spells lately. I think it is caused by his teeth. He is getting very strong. He can almost stand on his feet. He is a powerful boy. I have improved a good deal the last week. I have laid away my crutches and walk with a walking stick all about the house. I know you will be glad of this. I wish I could get your buggy as I could ride about some. Father could let me have his old mare now that his buggy is broke and he has not time to mend it now. Mr. Porter was here last week. He wanted me to promise that I would go and spend part of my time with him. I would like to do so very much if I had any way to get there. I want to go to see Ruth and stay a while with her and Mary, but I hate to ask for the buggy again. It is very lonely to be confined at one place so long. Mattie and help her knit you a pair of socks if you need them. I will try to send them to you have you given out all hope of getting to come home. I do want to see you so bad but it best perhaps for you not to come till you can stay for it would be so hard for you to leave your little boy and Wife again

## Keziah Stradley Osborne to Roland C. Osborne[6]

Beaverdam Feb 3d 1862

My Dear Husband

Something or other makes me feel very sad this evening. I hardly know what it is; perhaps it is because it is raining and dark; whenever it rains, I feel like I want to sit down by your side, by the fire, and lay my head in your lap, and talk to you; instead of writing I want a sweet kiss this evening so bad. I have been wanting one all day for I have felt bad. Somehow I have been dreading lest some evil was about to befall me; at least I felt that way until a little while ago. I went off by myself and tryed to cast my burden of real and imaginary cares upon the Lord and I felt that He would care for me. It seemed to me while I was on my knees I could all most hear the voice of my Heavenly Father saying It is I be not afraid. I will be with thee and bless thee and take care of thee. Only be still and know that I am God. I will try and trust my self and my Darling Husband and sweet boy to His care. I know that he will do right with me, however hard it may seem to me now. Thomas and Harriet and their children and Frances and Ruth and Feby have been here all day Feby is a Captain let me tell you a secret but you Must not tell it to anybody. Feby will have a little Playmate some of these days. Ain't that funny? Our sweet Boy is not well today. He has not been for a good while past I do not know whether he is seriously sick or not. I am all Most afraid he is. He is so dull and does not care to suck Much. I have been giving him some teas. If does not get better I will get a Dr.'s advice.

Monday Morning  I did not get to write much yesterday, so I must finish in a hurry this morning as I have a chance to send to the office. I know you want to know what I am going to do about going to see you. I have received your letters of the 19th and 26th. I was so glad to get them. I guess I am as glad to get letters as you are and I know I want to see you so bad as you do me, only you I know you want to see your boy so bad I do wish you could see him, but Dear I am afraid to take him unless he gets better than he is now. I don't think I can try to start for a few weeks any how; so you need not look for me by the 15th of Feb. Perhaps something may turn up before that time.  May be you will get to come home. I think that would be the better way if you could get off for I am afraid I can't go, but if you can't come I think I will try to go for I do want to see you so bad. I had a letter from Sister Addie last week. She does not want me to go very much on account of the baby.  I don't think she will go. Her sister Lou is in a bad state of health. You must not be uneasy about the baby. You know I will do the best I can for him.  Perhaps he will get better before long and then by that time you will know whether you will have to fight any or not. I think the Yankees will have to leave the southern climate before long I am afraid the climate will be to warm for you in the spring. Do try to take care of yourself Dear if you must stay there. Thomas is playing with his little girl. It is very fond him it makes me feel bad. My poor boy has no [Papa?] to play with him or notice him anyway. The girls Are very fond of him. They think there never was such a baby I suppose you have heard of the Death of General Zollicoffer and of the defeat of his army. It was a sad loss to the South. It reported now that there has been another battle in Kentucky in which the South gained the victory. I expect you know more about these things than I do. I hope you get your paper [Papa?] now. I am sorry you have such a wicked mess. It must annoy you very badly. You must try to live [line?] them down. Perhaps they will quit playing and swearing before you when they find you want join them and that you don't like to see and hear such. It seems to me that if the Confederate army is ever confede conquered it will be to punish them for their sins. It seems that they are getting worse and worse. But I guess the Northern army is as bad. But that does not excuse our men. [Heps?] had letter from [Lo?] last week. He had been in the hospital but was getting better. It is thought that their Regt will have hot work before long. [Lo?] says if there is any fighting to be done he wants to be in it. Brother John resigned his position as Lieutenant in the company he was in at first and sent home and raised a company for himself. He is the captain now. I think he is in Knoxville drilling his company. I have made you some pants and I don't know how to get them to you. If I was sure you would get them I would send them by the stage. I would love go and take them but I am afraid you will need them before I can go. I could not get velvet to make strips for them but I did the best I could. We can hardly get any thing here now. I hope they will fit you.  I cut them like your others and lined them in the seats and knees to save you patching What boys was it talking about [Heps?] I guess it Jud Heren or Thad Hyatt. Ain't I good at guessing if it was a right clever fellow and he will behave himself right nice and let them nasty black gals alone. I will let him leave her if the old folks are willing to it. Won't you feel right funny asking the old Man for his gal again.  You recollect you [gave?] her up when you went off, and you will have to ask for her again. Will you do it running like you did before. I guess you want be so bashful again. I had like to have forgot to tell you that we had a little snow last night. It was the first this winter. It looked right strange. It has nearly all melted off. I think there will be more soon. Come up and hunt rabbits a while. You have hunted Yankees long enough. They are so wild you I think will never find them. Matt has been letting Rufus pull my paper out of my hands. I kissed him on both cheeks for Papa. I love his Papa and I want him to love him too. You ask if he can sit alone. Not quite. He can a little at a time and stands on his feet right strong. You ought to see him eat apples. He can eat a whole one scraped for him he will cry as soon as he sees one. There is a great revival going on at Hominy Church. Some 50 or 60 have joined the Church. I wish it would reach as far Locust Fields. I wonder if they will have Parham again. I hope they won't. I don't like to hear him and I know you don't. I wish they could get a good preacher there. You must tell Uncle Judson not to have Parham elected for you want to join the church when you come home. That would be a happy time for me. We ought to right ourselves so we could raise our boy right. So thinks you Wife.

## Keziah Stradley Osborne to Roland C. Osborne[7]

Beaverdam February 16th 1862

My Dear Husband

The day for writing to you has again rolled around and it is a cold wintry day. I wish I could be in some little warm room in S.C. with you today; or rather that you could be by a good fire in N.C. with me and Rufus. Don't you think we would know how to appreciate such a comfort to day. I guess we would not get lonesome. Well may be we will be so situated someday. But it seems a long time coming. I have been thinking since I wrote last week that I ought not to have spoke so positive [?] about not going to see you for I would go if you was sick or anything the matter with you at almost any risk. I hope I may never be called to your sick bed yet it may be the case and if it should be nothing that I could possibly overcome should hinder me from responding to that call. We had a right smart snow last night and it was so cold this morning that Father could not go to Asheville [Nashville ?] to preach to day so I will not get your letter to night. I hate that but I can't help it. I will hope that you are well today and as usual writing me a long loving letter. If it was not for your letters I don't know how I could pass off my time and then I love to write to you in return or you would not get such great big letters from me. I have not had a letter from Haywood for some time. I heard yesterday that your Father and Aunt Tisson was to be married next week. I don't know whether to believe or not. I think they might have let me know something about it if true. However I am not very much concerned about it though I know I know you would hate to have a mother that you could not like. I will take that back. I know you will never have a mother again. No not one like the one you lost. Yet you have not lost her. She has only gone before you and she has shown you by her example the way to Heaven. I sometimes think that her pure spirit watches over your camp and that she is a ministering Angel to her soldier boy, for we read that Angels are sent forth to minister unto the Heirs of Salvation; and if that is so why may not those Angels who attend us be the spirits of our departed friends. It is a pleasant thought, and one that should influence us at all times, to live as we think our Angels friends would like to have us live, or rather God commands us to live. Are you tired of my preaching. We had company last night, two volunteers from Col Coleman's Battalion. They are now in camp at Reems Creek Campground but are ordered to march to Tenn. next Tuesday. Their names is Kinsey and Kelly. I told the girls they had a beau apiece. They both knew you and said that Rufus was just like you. You may take that as a great complement for I tell you he is a good looking little fellow and so smart sometimes I fear that I will think too much of him but God intended us to love him through not supremely. I felt badly when I heard that your Reg was removed from N.C. but if you had have remained there I expect you would have seen harder times than you have done. We have heard that there has been a hard battle fought at Roanoke on our coast and that the Yankees took our entire force at that point prisoners. Gen Mark Erwin from Asheville is said be among the prisoners taken. It is said that our men fought two days and killed near a thousand Yankees and lost about three hundred themselves. I hope it is not so bad as it is now thought to be. We usually hear the worst first. I expect you get all such news before it reaches us here. Do you get the Tenn. Baptist now. I don't wonder that you find it hard to be a Christian. If soldiers are all as mischievous as those two who have just left here, and I know you are placed among some who are a great deal worse. You told me once that you would not care if I knew your whole history since you have been in camp, except one thing that you mentioned. Now if you do hold out faithful among so many wicked men, won't I be proud of my noble Husband and thankful to my Savior who I trust has washed [?] you in His own Blood, and who I trust will keep you in spite of all the temptations of your camp associates. Monday morning. It is raining very hard this morning; I have not got a letter as usual from you this week, but I will try to write as usual. I hate for you to be disappointed when you look for a letter from me. I guess a good many in your Reg get letters from Asheville. You know James Queen in Captain Gradey's Company don't you. Well he is writing to Uncle Sam Stradley's daughter (not the one in Summey's store) it is a sister of hers, and folks think they will marry when he comes back. Don't you think that will be a bad speck for her. From what I can find out about him he won't do to tie too at all. There is to be a big meeting at the Baptist Church in Asheville next week. I don't guess that I will go to it you know it would not do for my boy to cry in town and I would not leave him to please any body. My boy is a particular somebody in my estimation. I have been trying for some time to get his likeness taken for you but keeps raining so I can't go. I took him down to Mrs. Killian's last week. The first time I have ever taken him out visiting. He looked at everything along the road and never pretended to cry. I think he took cold as he has not been so well since then. His teeth are still troubling him I don't expect you would know his likeness if you was to see it, unless you was expecting it. He has grown so much since you left here. Tell me how you imagine he looks I have been asking him how he will like his new grandma I am afraid she is too stiff a Presbyterian. If it is so won't they all ways have a fuss on hand. I had rather have a Baptist Mother would not you I wish I knew the straight of it. I think they ought to let me know or wait till you get back. I guess Aunt Mira will leave there double quick. It will most break her heart she has long expected to be

Mistress of that House. It will be a sad disappointment for her. Poor old Lady. I think well of her but I can't help being amused at her sometimes. I have filled up my paper with my foolishness. You must excuse me this time I had nothing else to write. May God bless my darling Husband in the prayer of your Wife

## Keziah Stradley Osborne to Roland C. Osborne[8]

Beaverdam March 2d 1862

My Dear Husband

Yours of the 23rd of Feb came in good time. I very readily examined a bad letter from you that day. It was so hot I could hardly write up here and no wonder you could not where it was so much hotter. I guess you have been cooler since then. It was very cold here all last week. But it is pleasant again this morning. You know my health always fails in the spring of the year and I begin to feel it again now though I have no room to complain my health has been so good all winter. Rufus is not very well this morning. Nothing serious I hope. Only he like all other children is troubled with sick brushes. It is no [on, an, a?] wonder that he is as healthy as he is. He was six months old last Wednesday and weighted 25 lbs. What will you take for him per pound supposing get a chance to trade him. I am glad that your health is still good. I feel afraid that It will not be much longer if you stay where you now are I have been thinking perhaps you would be sent to the mountains to finish your term of service. It looks like the WNC men will have to come back to fight for their own homes. There is a company of Artillery now being organized to be stationed at Paint Rock that is not much over 20 miles from here and it is thought that Asheville ought to be fortified immediately. The Tories of East Tennessee are threatening to burn it down. I believe there are some men here who would see there country ruined and wives and children insulted and murdered before they would fire a gun. I am right glad that they are going to be drafted. I see that there are great efforts being made to get all the 12 months Volunteers to enlist for the war. I think there are good reasons why some should enlist for the war. It would let old Abe see that the South was not tired nor whipped out yet I do not think all should enlist for the war. I don't think you ought to. It looks hard for those who have served 12 months to have to enlist again to fight for the lazy cowards who have stayed at home making money all the time and who never intended to go. I would not care much if some of the stores in Asheville was burnt up. They are only oppressing the people. R B Vance's Reg have moved to Cumberland Gap. I am afraid they will fare worse than ever there has been about as many again deaths in that Regt as their has been in Clingman's. Many no doubt caused by an necessary exposure that the Col. might have helped if he had tried. I expect Brother Thomas will Volunteer shortly I do not know what company he intends to go in I don't know what will become of his family. I don't think he ought to go at all but he hates the thought of being drafted there are now 9 Stradleys in the Field that I know of and I expect that Brother Judson will have to fight on one

side or the other as the governor of Tennessee has called out all Militia. I
don't know which side he will take. His wife leans to old Lincoln's side and
a man follows his wife don't he. I expect you had better get me a Repeater
to fight with in case the rascals should come this way. There would be no
one else to fight here. don't you think I could do big work? you ask if I can
tell you any thing about making a crop I don't know any more than a cat
about any of your things Or whether you will have any crop started or not.
None of The Haywood folks have visited me since I came from there 3
months ago. They write sometimes but never mention such ubjects. I
suppose they tell you how your stock is doing. I never heard how your
bacon sold. I reckon we can trust to Providence for something for you and
I to live on. Your Father told me I might take my boy to old Ning
Edmonston to support. That was one reason why I told you last week that
I was not going back there until you come home. If you should never come
back I think I would try support my boy until he could make his own living.
I don't know why they should object to his being called Rufus. I think it is a
very pretty name. He knows his name now as soon as it is called. I am very
sure I shall not change his name to please any of them. He has never been
any expense or trouble to them. Hasseltine wrote to me last week to know
how my little Basil was you had better believe it raised my English. I know I
ought not get so mad but I can't help it I have tried to live independent and
to mind my own business since you left me. I am so anxious for you to
come back so we can have a cabin of our own and more. If you and I did
live in peace once and I think we could again if we had the chance. We have
an important work before us. I mean, training our sweet boy up for
usefulness here and happiness here after. I expect you will scold me for
writing you such a letter as this but you know I always say what I please.
The meetings I told you of at Asheville lasted until Friday night. 3 joined
the Church and several moarners [?] were left. Won't you soon know for
certain whether your Regt will be disbanded in April or not. I have thought
I would like to meet you in Greenville if I could but perhaps I had better
not think of it. Times are getting so hard. If it is not disbanded then when
will the full time be up. I am afraid you won't get off. I always listen for the
war news from the S.C. coast with the most intense anxiety. I was sorry that
you had lost another man out of your company. Be careful of yourself Dear
you know you are subject to fever admit would be apt to go hard with you
now you are so fleshy [freshly?] in a warm climate I pray that your life may
be spared to return to your native home and to make glad the heart of her
who has loved you and waited for your coming these many long long
months. When I get to thinking of these things I can hardly sit still to write.
I can hardly bear to wait any longer. Don't you remember telling me that I
must come out to meet you when you come back and that I must bring our
little boy with me, for you said you would want to see him as bad as you

would me. I often think of our long talks. We little thought how we would be situated and would have to talk of our boy on paper so long as we have had to do. I still hope that there is a better day a coming and that we will yet live to enjoy each others company and play with our boy till he gets large enough to Educate and make his mark in the world. May he be a good boy. Good night my Dear

Kizz

## Keziah Stradley Osborne to Roland C. Osborne[9]

Beaverdam March 9th 1862

My Dear Husband

Writing must be done I suppose, whether I have any thing interesting to communicate or not. I tell you at the start that my stock of information is very low this morning. I have not had a chance to send to the Office for a week past and so I have had not letters or papers and am entirely behind the news. I was sick yesterday but am about well today. My milk has made Rufus fretful and cross. He has not cut a tooth yet. I think he would feel better if his teeth were through. I tried to carry him out this morning and went as far as the stables. I guess I was glad to get back. I was so tired. You must hurry and come home to carry him out. He is so heavy and he is never satisfied when he is awake with out he is out of doors. I think it very health for him. I think you will agree when you see him that he has been well taken care of. That is if nothing happens to him. Last Friday was the coldest day we have had this season. We could hardly keep warm in the house. I thought of the poor soldiers in Tenn. and Virginia. They must have suffered a great deal I expect you found it very pleasant where you are. How do think you would like to live all the time in a warm climate. I have thought you would be likely to have better health if you could get good water. I don't think I could live in a warm country for I can hardly stand the spring season here. You know we need to talk about going to Florida to live I hope you will get entire [entirely] rid of your cough this winter if you do your time will not be entirely wasted as it regards improvement I read a letter from Jo [?] yesterday. He says they had a hard time getting to the Cumberland Gap. Had to lay out at night with out their baggage and now they have had to go into cabins with another Regiment. He thinks the gap is so strongly fortified that the Yankees and Tories will never be fools enough to attack them there. He says they have 20 pieces of Artillery placed so that they command the road for 4 miles in the direction the enemy would have to come to attack them they have about 5,000 men in the gap. He says the Yankees will hear loud thunder before they get through there. I do wish the Rascals could be driven of [off] four soil and we could have peace one more. I can't help being afraid that you will enlist for the war. I know that many will serve their country as long as it needs them and I honor their Patriotism, but I don't feel like I could spare you any longer than the 12 months you have enlisted for. A great many think you will go in for the war. I have not much hope of your getting off before your full time is out. It seems to me that you have been gone more than 12 months already. I want to talk to you instead of writing so I could hear you laugh. Don't you remember what a big laugh we had the last day you was here about the words you spelled wrong when you was writing. I have thought of that many a time and of other things we used to talk about. I think I would know your voice if I were to hear among your whole Regiment I thought of you while I was reading my Bible this morning And I wondered if you was not doing the same thing. I know you cannot be as quiet as I am yet I think your Bible must be a great deal of company for you and you could not have better company. Oh that we could read it together and kneel in prayer as we used to do. But thank God we can still pray for each other and for Rufus. God bless and [?] sweet kiss [?]

Monday morning. I received two letters from you last night and one from Sallie. She says she wishes you had sent Leander to their house so that they could have had him buried at their church and taken care of his grave. Thomas started to see him as soon as he got your letter but was too late he was buried. Sallie wants me to go and stay with her this spring. I am afraid my health would not be good there long but I would like to go and see here very [well]. Now I must try If I can answer all your questions. You ask what Rufus can do. It would be hard to tell all. He plays with the cats and dog. Clingman comes to his cradle and lets him pull his ears and stick his fingers up his nose and do any thing he pleases with him. They are great friends. I intended to have had his likeness taken today but it is raining. I have been trying for a long time. His hair is about half an inch long. I believe it will be red or very near it. If he could get hold of your hair or whiskers, you would find out what he could do. I have given him the note you sent by Cathey to play with while I am writing. I have preserved all your letters but that bad one. The girls would not be apt to give you a more impartial [?] account of his martress [?] than I do for I believe they think as much of him as I do. He is a general favorite with Grandpa and Grandma and all the family. We are spoiling him badly. I am glad your Father has written you such a good letter. Perhaps I have said too much you know it is my failing. I expected you would scold me but I only told you the truth about the buggy I don't know when I will go to Haywood. When you come back I reckon. I have not heard any thing about your over coat. I wrote to [C K/R] Mingus last week to see if the balance of the money due Joshua had or could be collected. I advanced the money for Joshua at Addie's request and I am afraid I will have to lose it or go back on Joshua for it. It was $8 that I lent him and I paid him $8 that you used of his and 10 for your subscriptions. Father was needing money and I let him have 10 he will give you credit for it. I have about 10 left after paying for your pants. That is as much as I need just now. I sold your shotgun to Gaines. He gave you credit for 20.00 on your account for it. I have not got any shoes yet. Can't get them for less than three dollars a pair. Rufus will need a pair and a hat if he lives till warm

weather. I am not needing any thing else now. I thank you Dear for your
kindness and for your good kind letters. I will send your things to Cathey's
store if I possibly can. You know I have a poor chance. I would be for you
to leave where you are if you could get a better place but I am affraid you
will get into more danger. As your time is getting so near out they try to get
their pay out of your Regiment. [T] W Roe has bought him a negro man for
800.00 may be your could get me a right nice woman while they are cheap
but the best plan would be to get out of debt first I guess. They can be
hired here now very cheap. You ask if you make as many mistakes as used
to do. You spell some words wrong yet that look sorter funny. But you
know I have no room to talk The old folks have forgot all about coffee. We
all like Rye better. That is us young folks. I would care [?] if I never saw a
grain of coffee again for my own use I believe. I have answered all your
questions that I can think of now. I would like to see Cathey but don't
know how to do it. You see I must quit write to me very often and pray for
your loved Wife and little boy

## Keziah Stradley Osborne to Roland C. Osborne[10]

Asheville NC March 16th '62

My Dear Husband

You see I have moved at last. I came here to Sis Ruth's last Tuesday. I tried to get the baby liking [likeness; likening ?] as I came through but the artist was not ready and it has been raining every day since so that I could not get up I am afraid I can't get it in time to send it to you. I will keep trying since I came here Judson went to Father's after me to take me to Haywood. He got my trunk and brought it in here but it was raining so that I could not go with him. He said he would send Mingus next week. I reckon I will go if the weather is suitable and the road so I can travel. I expect Pigeon is up there has been so much rain lately the roads are said to be very bad now. I received yours of the 8th last night. I felt like there was something wrong when I saw so much blank paper, and as I read it down tears gathered thick and fast in my eyes but I forced them back until I went to my bed by my self where I lay for hours studying and crying. I felt like you would never love me anymore as good as you used to do and never want to hear anything more from me. I know it was wrong for you wrote gentle and kind even this time. I do not think hard of you I know that you do not know all. If you did I don't believe you would blame me so much as you do now. you charge me with noticing little things too much, sometimes little things have sharp points. Don't you know they have I am only sorry that I did not bear all with out complaining; can you forgive me for distressing you with my little troubles. If I were never to see to you again I never would forgive my self for giving you so much pain. And now I will drop this un pleasant subject. I will try not to distress you with any more complaints whatever I may have to submit to I know you have troubles enough of your own and I would rather try to lighten them than to add to them so I try to bear all in silence. One thing I know I do love you, and my Dear little Rufus, sweet child, he loves his Mama dearly. He is a great deal of company for me. I love to watch his quiet sleep for I know that he feels nothing of the cares of this world of sin and sorrows. He has got one little tooth now. Felay [?] thinks a heap of him. Feb [?] says tell Uncle Roland to please bring him a little knife when you come back. I do hope you will get off in April, and not have to stay for three long long long months more. There are three companies nearly made up in Buncombe for the war I have no news of importance to write and as I feel sorter bad I will quit for this time. My Dear I have not one single un kind feeling towards you I daily pray that the great and good God to spare your precious life and to shield you from all harm and danger and bring you safely back to your unworthy but devoted

Wife. You did not say whether you was well or not. You must always tell me for I feel anxious about you

Monday morning the weather is still so bad I don't know whether you need direct to Pigeon or not till you hear if you say any thing about this.  Do it on [separate ?] [paper ?]

## Keziah Stradley Osborne to Roland C. Osborne[11]

Pigeon River NC April 22d 1862

My Dear Husband

As I promised you that I would write once a week I will try to do so though I have no news at all to communicate excepting little family matters perhaps that will be better than none at all. The River is up now and has been for a week so that we have not had any papers or letters. It is so provoking when we are so anxious to hear. I think we ought to build a bridge across Pigeon but so it is. We have heard rumors of a fight near you and we are very anxious to know all about it. I feel so bad when your letters fail to come. It gives me the blues in spite of all I can do to prevent it. Time [?] and I have been talking today about what a nice thing it would be to give Mr. Lenore's [?] company a diner when they return. Right when they had a diner before they started, when I think of the time for you all return I can hardly sit still and wait. Then it makes me feel bad to think how many brave fellows have been sent home in advance who have been utterly unconscious that they were among their native mountains again. I have had experience enough to make me feel sad, even when I think of returning Soldiers I allude to my poor Brother. His company, the Rough and Ready guards will soon be home, and I hear of many who are preparing to welcome them home. Some girls are [?]ing to be married then, and are anticipating a great deal of pleasure. But Eby Ely?] has long since been at Home. We will not have the joy of clasping his hand Welcoming him back. No, no sweetly he sleeps. Then rest on my Brave brother until the Resurrection morn I do not know whether my last letter has reached you or not. If it has you are anxious to know how Rufus is by this time. I am happy to tell you that he is mending. He has dreadful sore eyes. It makes me think of what you said of yourself. When he first wakes in the morning, he can't see one bit till I bathe his eyes. I saw Miss Sallie Cathey the other day. She says the baby looks more like you than ever. Since you was [?]ened. I begrudge Sallie that little chat [?] she had with you. I little thought when you went off that you would have to stay all the time without coming back to see me, and your little boy Well I hope and pray that the time is not very far off when you will be at home for though I can't walk with you like I used to do yet we can have many a pleasant long talk. I never saw vegetation so forward as it is now at this season of the year. It is pretty cold now and very wet. Farmers are very much behind hand it would do your very soul good to ride up Pigeon valley now and see how pretty and green the meadows and wheat fields look. It is said that there never was a finer prophet for wheat than there is now in the western counties. We hear that the Militia is all called out of Burnsville to fight the Tories in Madison. I hope they will not have to stay long. If they do I don't know what will be done for some one to make bread there. You see I am nearly [?] done you must excuse such a foolish letter from me this time. I want to quit writing to you and talk awhile don't you want to chat with your loving wife

## Keziah Stradley Osborne to Roland C. Osborne[12]

Aunt Mira sends her love to you. She says the baby does her to look at instead of you. She is glad you don't forget her

Pigeon River April 30th 1862

My Dear Husband

I felt a little better this evening so I left my boy, and rode down to Uncle Josephs, and spent an hour or two with them. It looked like going home, like I used to go last spring. I almost looked for you to come out and help me off my horse and kiss me, and say "why you have come back to see me again." But such was not the case. I tell you Dear I feel like I could live any where under any circumstances if you could only be with me and Rufus. I thought about trying to get you a substitute before you wrote about it. But I tell you I am afraid it will be a bad chance there is nobody to hire to do any thing. I have felt like more like giving up this last week than I have done for some time. One reason is I have not been well. The day I wrote to you last week I was taken sick suddenly, vomiting with high fever, produced by severe cold I thought. Dr. Allen came to see me three or four days and at last got his medicine to act. It has left me very weak, but I am improving I acknowledge I am low spirited. I don't think you will wonder at that. But I will do the best I can for the sake of our boy. Sweet child he is a little thing now he is one pound lighter than when I weighed him at Asheville nine weeks ago. Sometimes I think this home [house?] does not suit him and me. But I will stop such low talk and tell you something that is more pleasant. Your wheat looks splendid I think you will make lots of it. The clover below our house looks fine and green. They got done sowing your oats yesterday. I think they will be too late to do much good. I suppose they will plant you some corn. Don't you think they had better sell Duff [?] if you don't get to come home soon. He would sell for a [$] 151 or 175 now and you know he will soon be getting to old to sell so well it would be stopping the interest on your debts. I think your Father might spare him now for old Julia's [?] colt is dead. He will not have any young colts this spring but one. Your little colt has been nearly dead with distemper those two fillies are still here and I am sorry for it. Have you sent Father any money for them. I expect he needs it badly to get his crop made, though he never said so to me. Your Father says he will do the best he can to get some one in your place. He says for you not to offer for any Office but to keep your present place if you can. You will not be so much exposed and will have a better chance to get off. I don't want you change your place if you can help it. Uncle Joseph thinks this war will not last much longer. That is all my hope now. I hope you will get a furlough any hour. This law does seem very hard but I reckon it is a Military necessity and we ought to submit as cheerfully as possible. Let me know right off what sort of clothes you will need me to send you this summer. I will try to make them for you. I want visit a bout next week, my health requires it. I think I will spend the month of June on Swanannoa for I am not much account to work any way. I feel like I would soon see you. I pray that I may. Be a good boy. Don't get out of heart. There is a better day coming I hope when we will meet again. Your Wife and Boy

## Ephraim Osborne to Roland C. Osborne[13]

At home July 27 1862

Dear Son

I know it must have cost you some uneasiness to reflect on the long delay of your request, that I should write you in return of your friendly letter, but Joseph leaving home has thrown every thing upon me in the fields in addition to my jobbing, feeding, and riding [?] and shopping, I have been too weary to write at nights, but I consider this morning to begin this, hoping I may finish it some when, and by it convince it was not for want of a good will towards you no, no, I am pleased you get constant intelligence of all our matters from Kezia, and in return we have the joy of hearing from you weekly, we were very anxious respecting your fate at the Richmond battles, that awful struggle has made many homes desolate, and broken for life many a fond heart, but God sent his Angel and turned from you the missiles of Death, O how much gratitude and praise is due to his name, I think we offered up one grateful offering of praise to him who holds the Keys of Death and the Grave when we found you were not numbered with Dear, I hope your life spared may be devoted to his glory and you made a good Soldier of the Cross, constantly under Arms fighting the good fight of Faith, charging the foes within your own heart in the strength of the Lord, driving them back more & more daily, like Lincolns forces flee to the last bound of their territory. In the death of your substitute we have another strong showing that we must all die for ourselves at the appointed moment, Christ died for us to open to us the way to Eternal Life but we must die for ourselves, Corporeally to enter that life if we are prepared for it, I hope his Death may have a lasting effect on mind for good, and do good to all his commands under arms, many must be left behind at the close of the War, but more awful still many will be left out at the last great day, who have hardened their hearts after seeing and escaping so many strokes of God's judgment, to them the Christians Captain will say with his muster roll in his hand, Depart from me I never knew you, you never buckled on the Christians armour, never fought against sin and corruption, never show yourself decidedly and determinedly side, may God give us grace to get near the Cross and fight till we die. We have a full shew of your needs before the Lord at least twice a day. Be very guarded against evil associates, lest they try to hang to you, if you return home. May the Lord help you to make a full surrender of all to his Son Conquered by love, bristing you all to him, believing he will save all that come to him, and you even you among the rest. I suppose Kezia told you I had bought another Servant. I felt compelled I could get no help till the middle of April. I paid in land and troublesome notes, a good portion for him, and I have until the close of the year to pay or go aceper [?] into the Bank for the balance. I hope to have some pork, beef, and corn to spare. Your Father spent a night with us a few weeks since, his wheat crop is very sorry, Francis Wolf's crop was not worth cutting, our crop is as good as usual. This morning Kezia and the big baby are well, he walks alone Strong. Joshua has married his long selected Companion Sarah came to see us two weeks since, with Emma and the baby, she came in company with a Neighbor and family, they returned safe. We remain as ever

Affectionately Father and Mother.
All are well

## Gov. Zebulon B. Vance to His Wife Hattie[14]

In Camp near Statesville
May 18th 1861

My Darling Wife,

We start in the morning for Weldon and I set down tonight tired & chilled with the night dew to write you my last letter from this camp. I am still quite well but in rather low spirits at the way things are managed at Raleigh. I see a pretty determined purpose there to carry on affairs under a strict party regimen; none but [illegible] and secessionists will be appointed to the Offices; the old Union men will be made to take back seats and do most of the hard work and make bricks without straw. So be it. I am prepared to serve my country in spite of the small men who control its destinies. But many persons are disgusted, companies are disbanding and I fear the result unless a different policy is adopted.

My uniform has been completed and the men look splendid in it. We receive the praise evey where; many persons pronounce us the finest company in the state. The people of Statesville have been kind to us beyond description. My camp chest has been filled with cake & all sorts of good things ever since I came and such piles of flowers, you never saw as grace my tent. I have a trunk full of baguettes to send home to you when I get an opportunity. From the appearance of things I guess we will be sent on to Norfolk very soon - an attack is expected there momentarily and the sooner the better as we would be enabled to get away from there before the sickly months of August and September. Do not feel uneasy about our stay at Weldon - it is not at all a sickly place till latr in the season and then not much so. I will write from evey point.

I did not get your letter today and was greatly disappointed. I am always so anxious to hear from my dear wife and children - you seem more dear to me than ever since I have been called to peril my life for your defense. May God protect us all and restore us to peace and happiness once more.

I saw Mr. Woodfin, Shipp and various others going on to Raleigh today - they brought me no special news from home however. The election did not surprise me. I had a hope that the convention would be of such a complexion as to change the face of affairs but I suppose not. Let it go.

I am sitting in my tent now listening to the whip-poor-wills. I guess you and the dear babies are all asleep. I trust in God you may ever be allowed to sleep in peace. That no foe shall ever come near our sacred precinets. I think so much of you and all the dear pleasures & sunsets of home - our children, our garden, our flowers etc. And my dear old Mother, how does she do? And sister Ann, Laura, Hannah and all the rest. God bless and preserve them all. Tell them to write me when ever they can. It is so late I must go to my straw. I need several things and when I get to a camp where I am likely to stay any time I will send you to get them made & you can send them to me by express. No more tonight. Kiss my dear war like boys & accept assurances of my undying love and affection.

Z. B. Vance

Zebulon Baird Vance

## Gov. Zebulon B. Vance to His Wife Hattie and Son Charlie[15]

Kinston May 25 1862

My dear wife

I rec'd yours yesterday & was sorry to see you sad, though I fear I am greatly to blame for it. I ought not to write you such [factful?] & often gloomy letters. But somehow I cant help it; when anything troubles me badly, it relieves me to let it all out to you. I am happy that it is in my power to write more cheerfully. Though this news [illegible] have is not of much importance the aspect of things is decidedly better than they been for some time past. It is pretty certainly ascertained that the enemys gun boats can not get up the James River to Richmond. There are over 20,000 troops at Petersburg to prevent them operating on the south side of the James, whilst McCellan is almost certain of being whiped if he attacks Richmond by land without his boats. In the west, the whole country relies with implicit confidence on the glorious Beauregard who has 100,000 of the bravest men on the continent under his command. He is gathering strength every day & the impression begins to prevail that he will annihilate [Hallacks?] whole army.

Gen Banks has retired across the Blue Ridge to Fredricksburgh, having the road open for old "Stone Wall" Jackson into Maryland & Penn. He is going certain & it is said he will be joined by 30,000 Marylanders with arms in their hands. God grant it. My legion is thinning and will yet be as successful I think (I had a desperate spell of cholic night before last from eating green peas but am well again. I had yesterday another letter from brother and also a long and very affectionate one from sister Laura, the first I have had from her since the war began. I do wish darling you & she could become reconciled again for my sake.)

Col. Burgwyn has gone to Raleigh and I shall be very busy this week, but I feel better when I have so much to do, and am able to do it. We don't leave this place I learn some of the troops at Goldsboro will go to Richmond or Petersburgh soon but our Brigade will remain here. I fear Davids friend Mr. Bindull is now our Major. I enclose a letter for Charlie, which I hope will please him. Give my love to Mother & all. Keep cousin Ann Lizzie with you as long as you can. Kiss any my namesake & the other dear boys & cousin too! I would if there. God bless you all. As ever darling your affectionate husband.
Z. B. Vance

May 25, 1862
My dear son Charlie,

Pa rec'd your letter, and was very happy to read it. I was mighty sorry to lose poor Todd, I wanted to keep him for my children to ride when this war was over. I want you and brother David to be very good boys, obey your Mother, be kind to each other & to brother Zebbie. You are getting old enough now to be of great assistance as well as company to Mother, and whilst Pa is away you ought to try hard to take care of her and protect her in her lonely home. You write me that the yard and grass is mighty green & nice: Pa is glad to hear his dear ones have such a beautiful home, and you and brother will always remember not to break or injure the shrubs and flowers, but always to play in the walks or on the grass away from the shrubery. Goodbye son, kiss Mother & brothers & cousin for me & tell all the howdy for me.

your affectionate Father ZB Vance

### Gov. Zebulon B. Vance To His Wife Hattie[16]

Near Petersburg
Aug 'st 4th[th] 1862

My darling,

The election is all over and if I only knew what was the result I could tell whether or not I would be with you soon. I have every assurance that I will be governor by a large majority, but it is not certain. From 38 regiments in the army I have rec'd more than two to one. But enough. I will be satisfied anyway.

We have been in a constant state of excitement here by the Yankee landing on this side. We have prepared for battle every day, marched, counter marched etc and finally found out that the Yanks were only plundering along the coast under cover of there gun boats & were not advancing as we at first supposed. Major Kendall has resigned & Col. Burgwyn gone home sick so I have it all to do. I think I shal be with you by Saturday, the 17th if all things go right or a few days further, at least not beyond the 20th God grant it. I continue quite well but feel fearful that a return to an indoor life will give me fever. I hope to find you & the children quite well & I know you will be happy. I got your letter of the 31st, am glad to hear my likeness gave you such a pleasant surprise - it is not a good one but I thought you would like it. I hope to show you the original soon.

Kiss my brave boys, love to Mother & God bless you all. As ever yours

Z B Vance

## William Williamson to Gov. Zebulon B. Vance[17]

Goldsboro N.C.
Jan. 6. 1863

His Excellency
Z. B. Vance
Govr. of N.C.

Dear Sir:

I engage you 2000 lbs of pork to be delivered here tomorrow or next day. It will be sent up with a lot of Government pork to Dr. [Haggs?] and you can settle with him for it @ 25 [cents] per pound. Did you ever expect to see the day a "Bunkum" man would have to pay 25 [cents] for pork? Please present my regards to Mrs. Vance and believe me

Very truly yours

Wm. Willimson
Jany. 6th 1863

**Birthplace of Zebulon Baird Vance. Buncombe County, NC.**

## Robert B. Vance To Gov. Zebulon B. Vance[18]

Shelbyville, Tenn.
Jany 28th 1863

Dear Brother:

      Your letter afforded much pleasure, and bro't vividly to mind times that are past & gone never to return. In all the ups and downs that have befallen us in this life, I have never forgotten our boyhood. The old farm & orchard, the paring French Broad, the rocky mountains, the fishing frolics and mad swimming spells in the river-these all occur to my mind often, and I think how changed things are now. When I was a child, I tho't as a child & spake as a child, but now that I am a man, I have put away childish things. Previous to getting your letter I had written you touching the Brigadiers place, stating that the 39th N.C. was with me. Since then I have also asked for the 60th N.C. approved by Maj. Gen. McCown & I judge by Gen. Cheatam, comdg our corps at present. I am obliged to you for getting the Legislature to interfere, altho the petition may not carry the point. A letter from you to Genl Bragg would have weight. If it did not get my Brigadier commission, it would at least (I think) keep me in command of the Brigade.

      We have no news of importance. There was a pretty warm firing this morning on Mufreesboro pike, but what caused it we cannot tell. Morgan, Wheeler, Forrest & Wharton are on the Alert & it will be hard to trap them. The Yankees will find it difficult to advance now, as the roads are awful. This shows the wisdom and sagacity of Gen. Braggs, movements. It would seem as if our falling back was unfortunate, but I think it was wise. The enemy to Murfreesboro had fine pikes from all diorections & was closer to his base. Here he will soon strike dirt roads & the worst in the world, besides the country is eat up. Well we are of necessity now a defensive army, and when the enemy advances he will have to bring his supplies 55 miles, which is a heavy job & gives our cavalry a chance to give them "fits." So mote it be. Gen. Bragg's head qrs/are/ at Tullahonia Tenn. I am very pleasantly situated now - have a nice tent, stove, bedstead, table & c. and a fine Adjutant General, John Davidson is near by & is cheerful as ever. Harvey is at Murfreesboro sick & wounded. I will write again soon. Judge Davidson says never mind that "waning"; that all will be right. Go ahead as you have begun & my word for it all will be right. Tell sister Hattie to write if you are busy.

My love to all
Affectionately  Robert

## A Friend to Gov. Zebulon B. Vance[19]

Morganton, N.C. Jany 29, 1863

To Gov Vance


Dear Sir

What is everybody's business seems to be nobody's & therefore I write to inform you that unless you depose the Col., Lt. Col & Adj of the militias of Burke the ends of justice will not be attained. They are inefficient & incompetent for their posts. To the end that you will be satisfied of the fact charged against them institute inquiry by sending an efficient officer & he will satisfy you that the present incumbents hold their commissions only to keep them out of the ranks of the [conscripts?].

The south mountains near Morganton are filled with deserters & hiding conscripts & have had recently daily accessions to their numbers. They are committing depredations upon the citizens in the flat lands & bold in their threats & unless soon routed or taken will be a serious evil to this community & the adjacent country. To show you that the Col. is either ignorant or wilfully guilty of neglect of duty, about a week or ten days since he issued an order for a detachment from each captains Co. to meet him in Morganton for the purpose of going to the south mountains. The day arrived, the men came but Col. Hilderbran did not make his appearance besides all this, his orders are issued in a way that the deserters [illegible] know precisely where he proposes to go after them. I might state many other errors of his but hope you will adopt such measures as in your better judgment will be successful in serving the St. Mountains & taking up these refugees from justice & putting to fight in our army. 50 or 75 men could very easily route them commencing at [Brindletown?] & the High Peak. The militia here are ready & willing to do ther duty if they had a leader that was competent.

This Col. Hilderbran was elected over competent men because he was a Democrat. I have given you the facts as they do really exist. I will be in Raleigh before a great while & will call & give you my real name. Do exercise in the mean while your authority & oblige many friends.

Your personal friend

Buncombe County Collections

1. C.C. McPhail letter to Thomas L. Clayton, 19 Dec 1863. Clayton Family Papers (1855-1922), #4792. Southern Historical Collection, Louis Round Wilson Library, University of North Carolina at Chapel Hill.

2. Emma Clayton letter to Thomas L. Clayton, 24 April 1864. Clayton Family Papers (1855-1922), #4792. Southern Historical Collection, Louis Round Wilson Library, University of North Carolina at Chapel Hill.

3. Thomas L. Clayton letter to Emma Clayton, 22 Sep 1864. Clayton Family Papers (1855-1922), #4792. Southern Historical Collection, Louis Round Wilson Library, University of North Carolina at Chapel Hill.

4. Keziah S. Osborne letter to Roland C. Osborne, 1 Jan 1862. Roland C. Osborne and Keziah S. Osborne Civil War Letters. Hunter Library Digital Collections, Western Carolina University, Cullowhee, NC.

5. Keziah S. Osborne letter to Roland C. Osborne, 12 Jan 1862. Roland C. Osborne and Keziah S. Osborne Civil War Letters. Hunter Library Digital Collections, Western Carolina University, Cullowhee, NC.

6. Keziah S. Osborne letter to Roland C. Osborne, 3 Feb 1862. Roland C. Osborne and Keziah S. Osborne Civil War Letters. Hunter Library Digital Collections, Western Carolina University, Cullowhee, NC.

7. Keziah S. Osborne letter to Roland C. Osborne, 16 Feb 1862. Roland C. Osborne and Keziah S. Osborne Civil War Letters. Hunter Library Digital Collections, Western Carolina University, Cullowhee, NC.

8. Keziah S. Osborne letter to Roland C. Osborne, 2 Mar 1862. Roland C. Osborne and Keziah S. Osborne Civil War Letters. Hunter Library Digital Collections, Western Carolina University, Cullowhee, NC.

9. Keziah S. Osborne letter to Roland C. Osborne, 9 Mar 1862. Roland C. Osborne and Keziah S. Osborne Civil War Letters. Hunter Library Digital Collections, Western Carolina University, Cullowhee, NC.

10. Keziah S. Osborne letter to Roland C. Osborne, 16 Mar 1862. Roland C. Osborne and Keziah S. Osborne Civil War Letters. Hunter Library Digital Collections, Western Carolina University, Cullowhee, NC.

11. Keziah S. Osborne letter to Roland C. Osborne, 22 Apr 1862. Roland C. Osborne and Keziah S. Osborne Civil War Letters. Hunter Library Digital Collections, Western Carolina University, Cullowhee, NC.

12. Keziah S. Osborne letter to Roland C. Osborne, 30 Apr 1862. Roland C. Osborne and Keziah S. Osborne Civil War Letters. Hunter Library Digital Collections, Western Carolina University, Cullowhee, NC.

13. Ephraim Osborne letter to Roland C. Osborne, 27 Jul 1862. Roland C. Osborne and Keziah S. Osborne Civil War Letters. Hunter Library Digital Collections, Western Carolina University, Cullowhee, NC.

14. Zebulon B. Vance letter to Harriet E. Vance, 18 May 1861, Zebulon Baird Vance-Harriett N. Espy Vance Letters, 1861, NC Digital Collections. State Archives of North Carolina: Civil War Collection.

15. Zebulon B. Vance letter to Harriet E. Vance and Charlie Vance, 25 May 1862, Zebulon Baird Vance-Harriett N. Espy Vance Letters, 1862, NC Digital Collections. State Archives of North Carolina: Civil War Collection.

16. Zebulon B. Vance letter to Harriet E. Vance, 4 Aug 1862, Zebulon Baird Vance-Harriett N. Espy Vance Letters, 1862, NC Digital Collections. State Archives of North Carolina: Civil War Collection.

20. William Williamson letter to Gov. Zebulon Vance, 6 Jan 1863, Zebulon Baird Vance (1830-1894) Papers, 1863, NC Digital Collections. State Archives of North Carolina: Civil War Collection.

21. Robert B. Vance letter to Gov. Zebulon Vance, 28 Jan 1863, Zebulon Baird Vance (1830-1894) Papers, 1863, NC Digital Collections. State Archives of North Carolina: Civil War Collection.

22. Letter from a Friend to Gov. Zebulon Vance, 29 1863, Zebulon Baird Vance (1830-1894) Papers, 1863, NC Digital Collections. State Archives of North Carolina: Civil War Collection.

# 3. BURKE COUNTY COLLECTIONS

## <u>Avery Family of North Carolina Papers, 1777-1890, 1906</u>

Waightstill Avery (1741-1821) of Groton, Connecticut, was the first of the Avery family to settle in North Carolina. He graduated from Princeton in 1766 and came to North Carolina to practice law. In 1772, he was elected to the provincial assembly and was appointed attorney general for the Crown. He resigned his position as the attorney general for the Crown in May 1776 and became North Carolina's first attorney general in 1777. Avery built Swan Ponds Plantation in Burke County. After the Revolution, he continued to practice law and was active in politics, representing Burke County in the House of Commons, 1782-1785 and 1793, and in the State Senate in 1796. Avery was challenged to a duel by Andrew Jackson in 1788 while trying a case in Jonesboro, Tennessee, but the disagreement was settled amicably by the two parties involved.

Waightstill Avery's only son, Isaac Thomas Avery (1785-1864), and three of Isaac's sixteen children are featured here: William Waightstill Avery (1816-1864), Colonel Isaac Erwin Avery (1828-1863), and Laura Mira Avery (1837-1912).

William Waightstill Avery attended the University of North Carolina and practiced law. He represented Burke County in the North Carolina House of Commons in 1842, 1850, and 1852 . In 1856 and again in 1860 he was elected to the State Senate. Avery was mortally wounded when he and Colonel Thomas George Walton led a company of Burke County militia against Tennessee Unionists led by Colonel George W. Kirk. William Waightstill Avery was brought home to Morganton following the skirmish and died on 3 July 1864.

Isaac Erwin Avery was born at Swan Ponds Plantation and attended the University of North Carolina. He commanded Company E of the 6th NC Regiment and was promoted to colonel in 1862. On 3 July 1863, at the Battle of Gettysburg, Isaac led two regiments against the Union position at Cemetery Hill and was struck by a bullet at the base of the neck and mortally wounded. He was buried in Riverview Cemetery in Williamsport, but after the war his body was moved without his family's consent to a Confederate cemetery at an unknown location.

Laura Mira Erwin was one of four sisters of William Waightstill Avery and Isaac Erwin Avery. She never married.

Captain John A. McPherson fought in Company E and was present at the Battle of Gettysburg when Colonel Avery was killed. McPherson writes a letter to Avery's father, Isaac Thomas Avery, to tell him of Colonel Avery's last days and last moments. In 1895, McPherson and Avery's brother, Alphonso, traveled to Williamsport to locate the grave of Colonel Avery. They were never able to find where Avery's body rested.

## Eliza Murphy Walton Letters, 1834; 1861-1863

Eliza Murphy Walton (1820-1886) was the daughter of John Hugh Murphy and Margaret Avery Murphy of Willow Hill Plantation in Burke County. She attended school in Pittsborough, N.C. and married Thomas George Walton (1815-1905). Thomas George Walton served in the Confederate Army in eastern North Carolina and retired as the Colonel of the NC 8th Home Guard.

## Thomas George Walton Papers, 1779-1897

Thomas George Walton (1815-1905) was the son of merchant Thomas Walton and Martha McEntire Walton of Morganton, NC. He was appointed president of the board of directors of the Morganton Branch of the Bank of North Carolina in 1859. During the Civil War, he served in the Confederate Army in eastern North Carolina. He was appointed vice president of the North Carolina Agricultural Society in 1871, director for the Eastern Division of the Western North Carolina Rail Road in 1873, served in the North Carolina House of Commons (now the NC House of Representatives) and was a trustee of the State Hospital for the Insane in 1897. Walton was married to Eliza Murphy Walton.

Thomas George Walton built Creekside in 1836. He and his wife Eliza Murphy Walton raised eleven children there. At the end of the Civil War when Stoneman's Raiders swept through western North Carolina, Colonel Walton met General Alvan Gillem and his troops on the front steps of Creekside to ask that Gillem respect his home and his family. Gillem and his men headquartered at Creekside during this period.

Colonel Walton served in the Confederate army with two of his sons, James Thomas Walton and John Murphy Walton. James (nicknamed "Jink") was wounded at the Battle of Chancellorsville. John (nicknamed "Jock") was wounded and hospitalized at the Battle of Appomattox. He escaped from his hospital bed to avoid surrendering to the Union and made his way back to Burke County from Appomattox County. His diary is part of the Southern Historical Collection at the University of North Carolina at Chapel Hill.

## Poteet-Dickson Letters, 1861-1902

Francis Marion Poteet (1827-1902) was a miller who lived in the Dysartsville area of McDowell County. He was conscripted in 1863, serving as a private in Company A, 49th NC Infantry. His wife was Martha Hendley Poteet (1826-1902). The Poteets had thirteen children. Francis and Martha Poteet both died in April 1902.

**Swan Ponds built by Waightstill Avery. Burke County, NC**

## Isaac Avery to Laura[1]

Camp near Winchester Va
Octo. 18 1862

Dear Laura

James Parsons arrived here a few days ago since and from what he said, I was very uneasy about brother Moulton. I was quite relieved when I got your welcome letter today, tho I still have some little apprehensions about him. I am very much distressed to hear of the situation of poor Nonie. It is with a good deal of difficulty that an officer can get leave to be absent from his Regt, even for a day. Thomas Alson [?] succeeded in getting another leave day this made 2. I was again disappointed about seeing Willie. Their Brigade (Branchs) had been ordered off on fatigue duty (tearing up R. Rd track) several miles and Alphonso could not get there. He learned from sick men that Willie had been in camp and went with the Regt on horse back. He did not hear from Albert. If he could have seen Willie he would have advised him to send Albert home. My boy Albert has been complaining for several days. I hear nothing more about small pox. The Brigade in which it was prevailing has been sent to the rear in quarantine. I have had all my men re-vaccinated.

Day before yesterday I recd an order not to allow any one to leave camp limits as we were likely to be ordered to march at any moment. At 1 oclock am yesterday we had an order to prepare three days rations & be ready to march at day light. Laid on our arms all day when after dark we got a message that "there would be no move." This morning ordered to resume drill &c as usual. I have no idea what caused the sensation. I hear Bragg has met with a reverse as well as Van Dorn. It seems that this is the fighting army. It is the only army that can whip the Yankees.

I wonder what Jed Hardy is doing. Dr Holt has been appointed Genl Penders Brigade Surgeon. We need a surgeon very badly and I would have Jed appointed principal surgeon if I thought he would accept. I am very short of Officers. I haven't a single field or staff officer present. I heard yesterday that my asst Surgeon (Dr. Henderson) was better-likely to get well. I haven't heard nothing from Sergt Erwin.

I can not tell how long we will stay here or what is the object of our remaining as we are. We cant stay for a great while, for it will be impossible to subsist our army. I judge from the fact that we have had a hundred ambulances running for some time transporting the sick from here to Staunton, and from out tearing up the track and burning the cross ties on the Harper's Ferry and Winchester Rl Rd, that we will fall back soon in the direction of Richmond.

I am laying down under my tent in an awful smoke, which will account for the badly written letter. If an opportunity ever occurs, I would be glad if you would send my uniform. Give my love to all

Your Affectionate Brother
Issac

## Col. Isaac E. Avery to Major, 6th Regiment NC[2]

An officer of the 6th Regiment, North Carolina Infantry, Colonel Isaac Avery was mortally wounded at Gettysburg on July 2, 1863. As he lay dying, he scrawled these words in his own blood on a piece of paper to Major Samuel McDowell Tate:

"Major, tell my father I died with my face to the enemy."

**Colonel Isaac E. Avery**

## William Waightstill Avery to Gen. Isaac T. Avery[3]

Morganton, 11 o' clock

July 8, 1863


My Dear Father:

No letters or private telegrams arrived tonight, but news in the paper, announcing a victory for our army at Gettysburg contains very sad distressing news for our family. The papers state that Col. Avery of North Carolina was killed – it must be either Moulton or Isaac – one of your beloved sons has fallen I fear.

William Avery

**William W. Avery**

## John A. McPherson to Gen. Isaac T. Avery[4]

Genl I T Avery    Camp near Orange C. H. Augt 3/63

Dear Sir, on last evening I received a letter from Major A C Avery, in which he stated that Elijah had reached home, but unfortunately lost the letter which I sent by him. I am glad he lost it and, for the reason that it contained nothing scarecly concerning your son, I did not have time to write. I did not know that I could send the Conls. body from Gettysburg till about two hours before our train began to move and then it took all my time to get his coffin ready and his effects together. I hope Elijah did not loose his sword for I did a great deal of riding before I could find it. The letter Elijah lost was just a short note. I wrote you a letter about 20th of July and for fear that has been lost, I will write another giving the same particulars concerning your son. On 1st day of July we attacked the enemy near Gettysburg and I never saw men fight better or act more gallant than the men of our Brigade. Col Avery rode up and down the lines and some of the time he was on front of the brigade gallantly leading and cheering on his Brigade. We rode up to within 30 or 40 yds of the enemy before we ever broke their lines, but at last they broke and we drove them to the town. The Conl. reformed his Brigade on the rail road and then advanced beyond the town, where we lay in a ravine all night and all the next day. The Conl. was in the finest spirits I ever saw him, talked about his Brigade how well pleased he was with it. he spoke in the highest terms of the 6th, how well officers and men in that had fought. Capt. Burns poor fellow fell in the first evenings while gallantly leading his company, as he always has done. he was shot through the head.

That night the Conl. and myself slept under an apple tree with our horses fastened near by to the fence. The next morning we were all up early and expected that we would have to go into the fight early in the day. We remained in the same position all day, the sharpshooters kept up a brisk fire all day, so that a man could not show himself along th eline without being shot at. The Conl., Capt. Adams and myself were laying down on the side of the hill. The enemy's sharpshooters kept us uneasy all the time balls hissing all round us. The Conl. began to laugh and said that place was getting most too warm for us, and that we had better move, it was always the Conl.'s wish if he should be so unfortunate as to fall that it would be in a great battle. Late in the evening of 2nd July, Hays' Brigade and Hoke's were ordered to storm the heights on our front. The last words that I remember to have heard the Conl. speak was to his Brigade when he moved forward and they were these words, forward guide right, the Conl. intended to go in on foot called a courier to take our horses. I dismounted and went to the left of the Brigade. The Conl. afterwards changed his mind and rode in on his horse. it soon became dark and you could not see a man, but a short distance. I did not see the Conl. face if I had I should of went to him immediately, as it was I did not see him till after he was brought from the field. he never spoke after I saw him. Major Tate remained with him the first night and the next day, I stayed with him. I asked him if he knew me. I took his hand. he pressed my hand as though he recognized me. it was the only time he ever acted as though he knew me.

The Conl. died on the evening 3rd just after dark. I had been with him all day. he would eat nor drink nothing. I had two men with me I kept his wound bathed with cold water every few minutes. I gave him a teaspoonful of water but he would not swallow, and I gave him no more. That night I went up into the town to have a coffin made about eleven o'clock. I succeeded in finding some lumber had two men detailed from the regiment before I could get the coffin finished. I saw that our troops would fall back from the town and if the body remained till morning, where it was that it would fall in the hands of the enemy. I rode out to the hospital which was about three miles from the town got an ambulance and removed the Conls. remains out to the hospital. it was nearly day then, I lay down slept a few minutes, when the surgeon received orders to remove the hospital farther to the rear. Another hospital was established and it was then that I learned if I had a coffin that I could get transportation for the corpse. I went to a mill got some walnut lumber, had as neat a box made as I could, and the Conls. remains put in it. I did all in my power to get the Conls. body off for I thought it was my duty to do so, and had I not thought it my duty I should certainly should of made the same exersions. In the Battle of Gettysburg I lost two of my best friends, Conl. Avery & Capt. Burns. I know the loss of your son has been a soar and bitter trial to you, and not only to you, but all your family. I will say this that the death of Conl. Avery is the greatest loss the 6th Regt. has ever sustained. I hope you will not think I am speaking dispairingly of either of our former Conls. Fisher & Pender, for when Fisher fell we got Pender, when he was promoted we got Avery. he has also fallen but his place is not filled. I have a bundle of things the Conl. bought in Pennsylvania they are ladies goods if I had any way in the world to send them home to you I would do so. I fear the bundle will be lost or stolen. We are having very hot weather at this time as hot as I ever felt.

Yours very respectfully,

John A. McPherson.

## Eliza Murphy Walton to Thomas George Walton[5]

Creek Side    Dec 26th [1861?]

My dear Husband,

I received your letter this evening. I could not help but be disappointed at not hearing from you as you <u>promised from Statesville</u> except through a note to Mr. Pearson he sent out to me but I suppose your motto must be for the present "business before pleasure." I am glad to hear for your sake of your kind treatment upon the way and particularly of your comfortable quarters in Tent and good health. I thought of you much during the sleet and rain and upon Christmas you did not mention it. I think you must have forgotten it. This is the third Christmas we have been separated in 20 years. I felt quite sad. <u>My good kind</u> sister Flo and William came home with me from Church and stayed untill night. I am sure it will be a pleasure to know your voice is much missed in the responses. The girls decorated the Church quite prettily and the musick was quite sweet particularly to me as I was only a listener.

Mr Roberts spent last night with us. Wm Sister H and myself went to the head of the road to day to get Cedars for the Church yd. The cars came in without a passenger. Mr Fishers mules were going to Salisbury to be sold would not it have been well for you to buy a couple. Julia said she saw Less [?] Tate in Salisbury for a few minutes. I heard your men lost some whiskey by accident as you went on or rather through a mistake of Lieut. Avery's. All of our friends are kind. Pappy stayed with me the second night after you left and Ma has sent out saying I must come in to see her tomorrow. I know I will feel sad as you have always been there with me. I am doing my best to be cheerful all the afternoons are sad as the time draws near when you generally came home I can't bear to think this will last for twelve months but this is an old story and I fear you will weary of my common place letter  men are not like women  they are taken up with other things and are not so dependent upon their wives for happiness  it seems all a dream to me your getting up and leaving with a company  I can't believe it hardly now <u>how could you do it?</u> Mr Roberts said he don't it was necessary while there were so many young men would could be better spared than you from home and I wife like advanced your own reasons for so doing, don't you believe for a moment I am growing patriotic I am done with it I believe it all talk. What do you think will be the effect of Englands course I hope and pray daily a speedy peace for us and a return of my <u>dear dear</u> Husband to his family. I don't know whether you will read all my scribble but I want you to keep your promises to write  I will live upon your letters and don't stint me too much. Did you forget the change you were to leave at the bank for me or were your funds too low   I don't know whether postage stamps enough.  I asked Hugh what to tell "Pappy he says he wants him to come home and Billy Bethel he wants to see him" he is not alone in that. We heard that Mr James Patton died saturday night   Mr Roberts is expecting to hear by the next mail that his Father is dead   I have sayed all I can think of that will interest you and must beg you to write often to your own dear wife   all the Children send love to you

Yours devotedly
E.M. Walton

P.S.
Jimmy says write him as soon as you know when he must start.  Also let me know anything you want me to send you by him that you have forgotten or have found out you need   don't you throw my letters about where the boys may get them   Tell Willie all are well at home

## Thomas George Walton to Eliza Murphy Walton[6]

Camp Wyatt   May 2d, 1862

My dear Wife,

As an opportunity presents by one of my men going home, I write to acknowledge the receipt of the Box brought by Tom McEntire, for which I am much obliged, it remained in Wilmington several days after its arrival before I got it, everything in good order except the Rolls, the loaf bread was very little injured and I have enjoyed toast made from it very much, the butter is very nice, and a great treat to us who have been so long without. Please give my love to Lauretta and many thanks for the Ham, it came in good time for we were out with no prospect of getting any; we occasionally get some milk from a kind Lady living in the Neighborhood.  I believe I mentioned in my last that Henry Mott had joined the company, his father staid with us on Tuesday night, he is looking better than I ever saw him, he said he thought he would like to be in the army.  I like young Mott very much, he and Tom McEntire, Jink [James Thomas Walton] and Hugh Tate, will form a Mess, some 10 or 11 of my men have dissentery but are all recovering. I turned over the medicine chest to Hugh and he has been attending them since his arrival.   The detachment from my company sent to Onslow have not returned, and the General told me yesterday that he would order me and the balance there in a few days.  We are expecting Burnside daily and preparations are being made to receive him, two regiments passed down the river to Smithville to day, a telegraph line is nearly completed from Fort Fisher to Wilmington which will give direct Telegraphic communication with Goldsboro, it is to be hoped that Burnside will meet with more opposition at this point than the Yankee fleets did at New Berne and New Orleans. I am satisfied that wooden vessels cannot pass the Fort, and I think even iron clads will have a hard time of it, if our men fight as they should; I think it probably I may be with you by the 1st of June.  Genl French says that by the conscription act the company must reorganize, and I of course cannot hold my position unless I reenlist for the War, and you should know I have made a solemn pledge to you that I would not do so without your assent, and unless you do so, I shall be faithful.  My men are very much opposed to my leaving, and it will be a source of regret to me, but there are claims on me at home paramount to every other consideration, not the least among them after my own dear family, is the duty which I owe my Mother, she has been sadly afflicted in her old age, and my presence may happily soften some of the pangs of her declining years in these times so distressing even to the youthful and robust. I am very much afraid the taking of New Orleans and the coast towns will deprive us of two necessaries of life Sugar & Salt.  Sugar cannot now be bought in Wilmington at less than 24 cts pr lb by the barrel. Salt at $6. pr bushel. If you have any sugar left you will know how to husband it. I would have bought some at this high price but could not get transportation for it. I have no doubt it will be much higher in a few days unless a decisive successful blow is struck by our armies at Corinth and Yorktown, which I hope and believe will be the case. The papers say if Lovell succeeds in leading his Army so as to reinforce Beauregard in time for the Battle of Corinth, and enable him to crush the Northern Army the fall of New Orleans will be more than compensated.

My health and appetite is very good now and I am gaining flesh. I have heard indirectly from Jink since he went to Onslow all well, they have had no encounter with the Yankees yet. I met with one of Capt Hills company who told me that a gentleman living just across the White Oak River near them had proffered to give them 50 Negroes out of 60 if they would save them from the Yankees, this would be a find field for a Guerilla Corps to operate in; I received a letter from your Papa which I was glad to get and am much obliged to him for it. I will answer it shortly. I don't believe I ever thanked you for the nice pants you sent me, they fitted very well, and I keep them for particular occasions. I send by Pearcy some candy for the children. The blocks of wood is a puzzle which I thought Hal would like to work at, when properly put together it forms a ball. I also send Jinks daguerreotype. If you do not prefer the original I will send you mine instead of coming home. Give my love to all friends. Kiss all my darling children and believe me your husband devotedly

T. Geo Walton

P.S.

I had just closed my letter when your interesting letter, with so much about my dear Children and home was received. I had anticipated a good many of your queries as you will find. I recd a letter also from Mr Roberts on the Sug [?] question, he seems to be rather desponding in regard to our national affairs in consequence of the series of reverses our arms have met with, and speaks of my seeing sunlight when all is darkness. Until I become satisfied that our cause is bad and God has withdrawn his confidence from us I will not despond but confidently believe that eventually we will succeed. This is no time to despair, but on the contrary put forth our whole energy and determine to be annihilated rather than be made serfs—if this feeling only pervaded the bosoms of our whole people (as it does a large majority) the world in arms could never conquer us. The day is not far distant when good news will be heralded to the People of the South , or I shall be sadly disappointed. The Yankees have us at great advantage wherever they can use their Gun Boats, but wherever we have met them inland with any thing like equal numbers Victory has perched upon our banners.

I send you a quire of paper out of my small store, and will send you stamps whenever you need them.

Good night dear Wife
T. Geo Walton

**Creekside built by Thomas George Walton. Burke County, NC**

## Eliza Murphy Walton to Jock [John M. Walton][7]

Creek Side July 25 1864
My dear Jock

The second letter from you since you left Petersburg was received the 10 day of May. We were so glad to hear you were well also one from Jink he is safe tho he does not mention his health. I suppose it is good he had not been so fortunate as you in his first accounts of the raid as he heard our place was destroyed. You have not received Mary's letter written directly to you after your Aunt Lauretta's death. I hope you have before this as it gave you all the particulars. She seemed very gratified at you being so thoughtful of her and seeming so anxious about her. She was only rational at very short intervals for two days before she died. It was one of the saddest events of my life, only three sisters and one of them gone.

Eliza is at Mr Erwins & will spend the summer with them. She looks very badly. W. W. Avery died of the wounds he received two days after he made a will and left Alphonso his Esecutor, who is here now and intends on resigning. Uncle Moulton did not make a will and his family are troubled about getting someone to attend to his business. Lizzie is in great distress. Mr Houke was also wounded in the raid very badly. I hope we will not sufferer again as there is a Reg and 2 companies of cavelry here now and your father is appointed Col of the Home Guard. The Reg is the adjoining counties. The Cavelry companies pursued a band of deserters and Yankees and captured 27 of them a couple days ago.

Your aunt Mary has been very sick with the measles her recovering was thought doubtful for a few days. Mr. Caldwell also has them badly. Maggie is still at home & will remain a week longer. Miss Lounders is with her. Ella Erwin will return with them. Frank Craig and Tom McEntire were here at the time of the raid and gave all the assistance in their power. Frank has been sick ever since. Dr. Pearson was wounded in the knee and will be a long time recovering. Old Chandler Foster of the one in Capt. P- Company was killed.

We have had a very long dry spell, our gardens and fields are all suffering for rain very much. We have had splendid crops of black berries. I am glad to get milk and butter now. I know you enjoy it so much. Jink said in his letter he was going to Richmond on a pleasure trip. They are very near it now and said all the Officers had been nearby and they wanted to get away from the Yanks a while. Willie Avery's wound is very painful and he is very much reduced in flesh. I did not think you had much to spare when you left home. How do you look? How are your boots holding out? I suppose you got a supply.

Lola and Mary are going to town and will send a letter to you and ink to put in the office. I hope you will soon be at some place where you can write regularly and get letters from home. Hugh and Herbert are as bad as every. They are out all the time in the sun. Do write again soon. I will make May write you soon before she leaves home.

Your devoted
mother E.M. Walton

Have your daugerotype taken before you write again.

## Thomas George Walton to Eliza Murphy Walton[8]

Wilmington, Jan 16th,1862
My beloved Wife,

I have no doubt you have been disappointed at not hearing from me before this but I have had no opportunity of writing until now. We reached here safely on to day being six days on the march from Goldsboro we staid six days at G. by direction of Genl. Gatlin to refresh the men and horses, Jink [his son James Thomas Walton] and Stuart arrived the day before we left. I went immediately to the post office on my arrival here and found as I expected a letter from my dear Wife. I am relieved to hear that you bear our separation so much better than I feared. Your letter read at Goldsboro (by Jink) containing the love pledges of my dear children almost unmanned me for the time, kiss them over and over again for me and tell them how much Father prized their little missives of affection, and that I shall be disappointed if Mothers next letter does not contain something from them. I stayed last night with Mr. Hasell Burgevina (?) and sister. He lives 8 miles from Wilmington in a (?) of opulence and polish living in an ancient dwelling built in the Old English style by his Grandfather an Englishmen, the house is in a fine state of preservation and kept precisely as it was left by his ancestor, they are church people and great admirers of the Bishop. Lieut. Tate [Samuel McDowell Tate] and Avery [Isaac Erwin Avery], Jink and myself took supper with them, Tate and myself staid all night and enjoyed the luxury of a good bed, the sister Miss Sallie is a maiden of some thirty five years, not handsome but very intelligent and agreeable, she insisted on my coming to see them as often as an opportunity occurred, and Mr. Burgevina made me promise if Jink should get sick during our stay near Wilmington that I would send him to his house to be nursed by his wife and sister, his wife was not at home being on a visit to her relatives in Virginia. I paid my respects to Genl. Anderson today and am favorably impressed with him, he said he would do all in his power to give my troops as healthy a locality for our quarters as the vicinity afforded, and sent Major Lamb the Quarter Master with me to examine two localities and I am going tomorrow to look at another. I think we will be situated about 3 miles from town and perform such duties as the General may assign us, there is a good deal of sickness amongst the troops here principally measles and mumps, one of my men (Fitzgerald) broke out with measles to day. I sent him to the hospital by direction of the Genl. the balance are all well with good appetites. Flour is very high here worth $12 per barrel and difficult to get. Our baggage has all reached here safely. Stuart and Jink left it between Salisbury and Raleigh the conductor refusing to bring it on. I detailed Mr. Moore from Goldsboro, and he finally succeeded in getting it on. I have not had time to examine its condition but hope to find it all right. We are tonight in a large comfortable house in the suburbs, and I am now writing by a comfortable fire. Yesterday was the most unpleasant experience since we left home, the transitions from warm to cold in this region are sudden and extreme and this fact must make it in some degree unhealthy, the better class look ruddy and healthy while the lower look sallow and squalid, the greater portion of Duplin and New Hanover Counties passed over by us is miserably arid and unproductive, covered with the everlasting long leaf pine, varied by cypress swamps, the boughs of the cypress festooned with the long moss which seems to be the gloomy offspring of the miasmatic pools in which they flourish. The Bishop is here I have not seen him as yet but hope to do so tomorrow. In regard to Jocks going to school I hope you will send him where you think best I know he ought to be somewhere and hope you will impress the importance of his acquiring a good education upon him. I am sorry to hear Wm. failed in getting Claywell to take the house, tell him he had better employ Leigh or Shell to reroof it while it is idle, and to have the Ice house fixed up and filled if an opportunity offers. I expect you and Mr. Stacy [probably the overseer] will manage the farm matter, as well or better than it would be done if I was at home. I don't know when I shall get to see you dear Wife unless you come to see me. It would if anything could add to the pleasure to see my dear children but this I know cannot be now. There has been a great deal of excitement here growing out of a message rec'd from Senator Geo Davis of the place stating that Genl. Beauregard had telegraphed to Richmond that Burnside's fleet was (?) for this place, as he has failed so far to make his appearance the excitement has in some measure subsided. I do not see that the prospect for peace is more flattering than when I left, unless the financial difficulties in which the Northern (?) say the Lincoln government is involved, may have the effect. Reeves does remarkably well better than I expected, he and Lieut. Tate's boy cook for our mess, and I assure you do very well. Reeves makes better corn bread than we have at home, so far as wheat bread is concerned we have (?) chewed it, we have had fritters occasionally. I do not think we will need a stove until we get a house to go in. You may assure yourself that I will not subject myself to unnecessary exposure. Your letter was dated the 9th and I read it on the 18th. I will look for another from either you Mag or Hal today. I gave I.W. McElrath money to buy a barrel of yams for you. I hope he does so. I don't believe I have indulged in so many endearing expressions sweet wife this time, and if you don't like it you must blame yourself, as all the letters I have read from you caution me that others open and read mine. I don't see why you would object to Stan [his son Stanley Walton] doing so for I suppose he has no objection to his Father telling his Mother that he loves her as (he does) above all earthly things.      Truly yrs, TGW

**Colonel Thomas George Walton**

## Thomas George Walton to Eliza Murphy Walton[9]

Camp Anderson 3 miles East of Wilmington  Jan'y 23d, 1862

My dear Wife,

I have been much disappointed in not hearing from home this week, yours of the 9th (?) being the last I have rec'd and which I answered immediately. I hope to get one to day. We are encamped as you see by the heading within 3 miles of W. [Wilmington]. Genl. A. [Anderson] was kind enough to give me choice of three localities and after a thorough examination I have determined on this as being the most healthful and convenient, it is situated near the residence of an Old English Gardener who with his wife comprise the whole of his white family, they are very kind and he readily gave up for the Officers' Quarters a house which we find convenient and will be comfortable so soon as we get a stove, his name is Hopkins and from appearances seems to be skillful and tasteful as a Florist and Horticulturist, the old lady says they have a great many beautiful flowers in their season and the grounds are filled with rare evergreens. I am writing in his parlor by a good fire which I assure you is very comfortable today. The weather here seems to be very variable on Tuesday being so warm that most of the men threw off their coats being oppressed with the heat, but today (Thursday) and yesterday a strong North Easter has been blowing accompanied with rain of an icy coldness. I have been very busy superintending the erection of our stables which I think we can finish the 1st fair day. The men are still in tents but lumber will be supplied us, and we purpose beginning our shanties as soon as the shelter for our horses are completed. I have seen very little of Wilmington as yet, and found no acquaintances except among the Officials of the Army. The Bishop called to see me before we left town and invited me to call on him which I have not done as yet. I went to the church he preaches in twice on Sunday he did not preach in the morning but did at night, delivering his usual clear masterly style a most admirable sermon on the present crisis. I wish my dearest Eliza you could have been present, abounding as it did in consolations to those who have dear friends and relatives in the service of their country. The Bishop said he has not the slightest doubt the whole was directed by the providence of God and that the calamity and sufferings we are undergoing will be beneficial in their final results. That the returning of the people as a whole in the Southern Confederacy to the Lord their God repenting of their former sins would bring the war to a close sooner than if the navies of all Europe were to join our standard. We have not as yet heard of the destruction of Burnside's fleet. Genl. Anderson was under some apprehension that it might be intended for W. [Wilmington] and as we are encamped only 5 miles from the coast advised me to be very vigilant for fear of a surprise, tho' other officers seem to think there is not the slightest danger, I do not suppose we will be called on to perform very arduous duties until our quarters are erected, and we are instructed in some degree in the drill, a Capt. Haxall (?) was recommended for that purpose and I have accepted him, he is from Virginia and is one of the Genls aides. Tell Stanley I met with his friend Mr. Cotter who seemed delighted at seeing me, he stayed with us until 9 o'clock at night I told him that Stanley and Wm were coming to see us after a while and he seemed to be as much pleased as though he was going to meet a relation from whom he had been long separated, he belongs to a Cavalry Company gotten up very much in the same way ours was. I also met with Mark Erwin & Andy Shuford (Dr. Sudderth's father in law) I learned from Shuford that Mark has been very steady ever since he joined Green's (?) Battalion, they are located about 4 miles from us at Mitchells Sound. My Lieuts are behaving very well now and I think Willoughby will and has improved in his habits, W.B. Avery has measles and I think will do well he has taken a room with the Gardener and has very comfortable quarters, he seems to be low spirited today, which I suppose arises from the fact that (?) began in the same way. I see no reason for apprehending sickness here there is certainly no local cause for it very near us. Mr. Hopkins says it is the healthiest place in the world as he is satisfied from a twenty year residence without sickness. I begin to want to see my dear wife and children very much, but cannot at present make any calculation when I can do so now; do write every week as it is a great comfort to get your letters. Tell Hugh he must not forget (?) & Billy Bethel. Tell him everybody says Billy is the best horse in the Company. Tell George I had to let Jink have Ball to ride for the present, his horse being so much reduced by distemper as to be unfit for service for some time. I don't think I ever saw a horse suffer so much; he had to be lanced in four places and ran gallons. George Moore is a smart boy and very useful to his father they have gone to day to see the ocean, and I think will pay dearly for the sight as it still rains and is bitter cold. Tell Florence Father misses her good night kiss of affection, and I want her to kiss Mother for me every night as well as for herself. Tillie [daughter Martha Matilda Walton] must learn more pretty songs to sing for me when I (?) Lucy [daughter Lucy Walton] must keep dear Mother's spirits up by her frolicsome mimicry. Tell Mag [daughter Margaret Tilghman Walton] I won't send her a kiss until she writes to me, dear little Herbert [son Herbert Huske Walton] is walking. How I should like to ride him on my knee this evening. I send a messenger every day with my morning report to headquarters and get my papers and letters I will not close this until he returns with a letter from you I hope—

TGW

**Thomas George Walton to Eliza Murphy Walton**[10]

Camp Heddrick April 2d '62

My dear Wife,

I received your welcome letter last night and enjoyed it very much. I hope the next will come sooner and be longer; you will see from the station this is dated from, that we have left our old quarters. We left on last Sunday afternoon at ½ past 4 o'clock p.m. and reached here at 10 o'clock p.m., a distance of 20 miles, over a heavy sand road. I felt very reluctant to leave our old quarters after having done so much work in order to make ourselves comfortable, but am very well satisfied with that change, so far as I am personally concerned; the officers have very nice comfortable quarters, and more satisfactory than all, I have a room to myself which can be kept clean and private when I desire it. This camp is situated on the Cape Fear about 1 ½ miles from Fort Fisher and 1 mile from the ocean. I have not been to the Fort but understand it is very strong, having (?) heavy casemated or bomb proof guns and 24 not casemated there are about 1,800 or 2,000 troops here, Col. Iverson of the 20th Regiment is in command of this encampment and Major Heddrick of the Fort, they think there is no probability of an attack here shortly. 10 miles below us on the river is Smithville, the county site [seat] of Brunswick; just below is Fort Caswell. Our duties are becoming more arduous. I have just received an order directing the detail of 10 new noncommissioned officers and 1 Lieut. to perform picket duty covering a space of 12 miles and not to return to camp for 3 days. Jink, Bennett and McElrath are the noncommissioned officers and Kincaid commissioned they are in good spirits and seem to regard it as a mere excursion. I am glad to hear Mary is boarding with you (as you say) she will be a great deal of company for you, give her my love and tell her I hope she will become a good churchwoman, we can hear nothing of the movement of Burnside or the intention of our troops said to be 25 Regiments at Kinston, Col. Iverson thinks Burnside will attack them, if so I think he will get a thrashing. You must not be uneasy about me but have faith that God will preserve me to return once more to the arms of my dear Wife and Children. Tell Mag & George I have not rec'd their promised letters yet, I received a package of seed by Winn from Stanley which I sent to Mr. Saunders. There is not a drop of liquor in our camp now, and the Police regulations are so strict that it is almost impossible for the soldiers to get any. The Capt. (Howard) of the Cavalry Company who left these quarters the night we reached here was about to be court martialed for drunkenness, and resigned in order to avoid it, this warning will have a good effect on some of my own. We get the mail every day from

Wilmington by my own couriers, so you will continue to direct your letters as before. I am very glad to hear poor Sister has become reconciled somewhat to her sad misfortune. I know it is hard to bear but how much better than the 1st report she will surely appreciate give her my love and tell her to have confidence in Him who orders all for the best. Can't you persuade Ma to ride out and see you occasionally I am sure it would do her and you both good. I am surprised to hear the report about Vance's Regt, it is believed here by all that they fought with distinguished gallantry. I regret to hear that Mrs. Roberts failed to escape from New Bern, altho' I doubt if there is a woman in the Southern Confederacy who will be or is better adapted to foil and hold at defiance the Vandal Yankees than she. What does Mr. Roberts think of it, let me know if he hears from her, it would give me great pleasure to be so situated that I could strike a blow for her release. I esteem her very highly, I hope William will rent the house to one or the other of the parties applying it will go to ruin unless occupied. Tell Stanley to pay Winn's wife $20 he has placed the money in my hands. Jink says give all his love and he will send you his daguerreotype the 1st opportunity he has of going to Wilmington, and I will send you my own if you insist upon it. If you have an opportunity a little Butter will be very acceptable we have been out for 4 or 5 days and it is impossible to get any here. Stanley has not acknowledged check, sent by me to him by Perkins & Bristol. Write more about the children, their sayings and doings. Kiss them all for me and tell Hugh he must not forget (?) and Billy (?). Does Florence still kiss for me? Tell Tillie I will send her a better book next time; is Lucy as full of fun as ever? I would like a little of it this morning; are the services of the church well attended now. Tell George he must sit in my place and remember to behave himself well. Tell Wm. to pay Miss Kate whatever amount of my Rutherford funds he has in her hands, present my regards to her and give my love to all my dear relatives. I know you remember me in your prayers my own dear Wife. God preserve and bless you.

Yours devotedly,

T. Geo Walton

## Thomas George Walton to Eliza Murphy Walton[11]

Camp Wyatt
April 9th, 1862

My dear Wife,

I made Jink answer Mag's letter immediately, I have not received one from you since but hope I shall to day. I have not left the Camp since we came here, it is twenty miles to Wilmington and I do not know when I shall have an opportunity of going there. I am under the immediate command of Col. Iverson of the 20th Regt. and have not the control of my time as when you were with me. We have just received the news of the Glorious Victory achieved by Johnston & Beauregard in Tennessee [Battle of Shiloh, April 6th], a few more such and the dark cloud which has recently lowered upon us will vanish and the Vandals of the North will be forced to ask for peace. It is believed that very few of the whole Federal force will escape amounting to 35,000. This will enable us to get back all the prisoners they have of ours and a number to spare. I suppose you will have rec'd by the papers all the details before this reaches you. I will send you the Journal the 1st time I go to Wilmington. I do not think there is much prospect of a fight here at present altho' the Yankee Vessels are frequently seen lying off out of range of the guns of Fort Fisher. 5 passed within sight on yesterday. The defenses here I think very good there are 29 heavy guns in Fort Fisher and the batteries adjoining six of them casemated or bomb proof. The Fort is immediately on the beach of the ocean about ½ mile from the river, just across the Inlet (commanding it) is Zeke's Island with a battery of 11 guns about 3 miles up the river on the Brunswick side is another battery mounting 10 guns and a long line of entrenchments this was originally the site of the old town of Brunswick burned by the British, the walls of an old English church are still standing, within the walls trees are growing two feet in diameter. I crossed the river in a boat yesterday to see it. I learned while there that an old acquaintance Dr. John Hill lived only 2 miles off. I think I will go to see him the 1st leisure day and get a good dinner. We are living pretty hard about now, and I am getting very tired of fried meat and rye coffee. If Hugh Tate comes down try and send me a box by him with some butter & cheese. Tell George one of my men bought a fine turkey, and as we were going to practice at target shooting 100 yards, offhand he proposed that the best shot should have the turkey, and I won, very nearly striking the center. Our men are elated with the anticipation of a good dinner off of him next Sunday. It is strange dear Wife that you and I should be suffering at precisely the same time with severe cold. I don't think I ever had so severe a one in all my life before. I am now however much better, in fact almost well and I have not been confined to my room at all. I am anxious to hear that you have entirely recovered, and if I do not get a letter to day will be uneasy. I have heard nothing from Tom McEntire since he left I suppose he will be here shortly, let me know if he has been to Burke. This is a very unpleasant day heavy wind with rain since midnight. I don't see that vegetation is at all more advanced here than it usually is at home at this season, this is a very desolate region occupied entirely by Pilot and Fishermen the land is scarcely tilled at all, and there seems to be but little difference so far as appearance goes between the seasons, evergreens being the principal growth and the ceaseless roar of the ocean being always the same. I paid Mr. Saunders my bill it was very moderate only $8. The Kincaids paid Ivy $13 apiece. I am sure I never paid a bill more cheerfully and feel very grateful for their kindness to us. I hope dear Wife it will not be long before I can come and see you and all my dear friends. I believe with you that the war will end before the year is out, but not with a subjugated South, this cannot be, we would be unworthy of our birthright was it so. Our cause is just and I have faith that God will answer the prayers of his people which are daily made for the success of our arms; I miss the services of the church here very much, there is a chaplain in the Regt but he has not preached since I have been here, he is a Methodist. Tell Mr. Roberts he has never written me the promised letter about the jug. The water here is very bad and I should be sorely tempted to mix it occasionally if I had the means of doing so, but I think the whiskey blockade much more effectual than the Lincolns, jesting aside if you send me a box tell Stanley to put in a flask to be used in sickness. My command are all well except Laxton [Dr. Joseph Lavender Laxton] who is quite sick with chills. I fear he will not be able to render much service this summer. I do not like this locality much and hope we will be sent some somewhere else before the warm weather begins. I am glad to hear Eliza and her babe are doing well. If you want money tell Stanley to let you have it, tell him to get a statement from Mr. Erwin of the amount I have in Bank, say to Mr. Stacy to get in every foot of land he thinks will make corn. His son has been a little unwell but is better. Tell Florence I want to see her very much, your next letter must be a long one everything about home is doubly interesting to me now. It is almost time for the couriers to start and I must close this uninteresting sheet was it not that it conveys to my dear sweet wife the intelligence of the health and unabated love of her husband.

T. Geo. Walton

P.S. Give my love to all my dear friends & relatives. I have not rec'd a letter from any one of them except you & my children since I left home.   TGW

## Peter Poteet to Francis M. Poteet[12]

July 16, 1861

My Dear brother

I am happy to inform you that I am still spared to the present time to drop
you a few more lines to let you know that I am Well and I Do hope that
these few lines may Reach you and find you all Injoin good helth for I find
that It is one of the greatest Blessings that We Can injoy on this earth I Was
happy to receive your kind letter today for it dose me somutch good to here
from eny of my People in this troublesum place Whene I study so mutch it
appears To me that I Cant stand it some times But yet I do hope & pray
that I may live to git home Again But it is doutfel About that  I have scaped
thousands of balls onst But the next Battle may take thousands of us  there
is no telling about that  We ar expecting A fearful Battle at this place every
day and When it dose Come off it Will be one that Will be long emembered
By them that escapes  But We ar Well prepared for it and at work Every day
you said somthing about our battle being at harpers ferry hit was 15 miles
below here At aplace cald bethel Church they was meny Balls Went into the
meting house  our old Colonel Was in all of the mexicin War And he says
that he never saw such abattle in his travels they ar fiting about here every
day or two  I got aletter from henry poteet a day or two ago and it was
Amity good letter  I am glad to here from you all & here that all of you ar
praying for me and for all I Want you to give all of the nabors my best love
& respects  tell my Pore old mother howdy for me And perhaps farewell
for this May be the last letter that I ever May have the Chance of riting to
eny of you  my feelings Was Mortyfide & the tears Brock from My eyes
When I Was reding your letter & Come to When it told Me of the death of
Mr Suttle for I thought more of him than any Man that I ever saw in all of
my travels But if I Can go Just as I think he Went I think that I Would go
happy there is a pour of sickness here at this time and agreate many Deaths
We haint lost many men out of our Company yet and I hope that We will
all live to git home again  Rite to me Assone as this Comes to hand And
direct your letter to the Same place that you did the other so nothing more
at present only Remanes your affectent Brother till Death

Peter Poteet to F. M. Poteet
And family and
Mother Brothers & Cister
May the Lord bles & save us all is my Prays amen

## Peter Poteet to Francis M. Poteet[13]

August the 7, 1861
Yorktown VA.

Dear Brother

I again take the opportunity of Trying to Rite to you to let you know that I
Received your kind and loving letter in dew Time and was glad To here
from you all and here that you was all well  I would have Rote soner But I
have bin sick for 3 weekes & was very low When I Received your leter & I
am bad of yet But I do hope and pray that I may git well And live to return
To my desolate famley onst More  there is about half of our Company sick
at this time and some of them is Bad of there was One of our Company
departed this life last knight And it is to Be hoped that he is gone to rest
where there will be no Battles to fight nor no lamenting to git home But
where all is Well  he was a young Man by the name of harrison avry a son
of James avrys And I think he was a good boy & herd some of our men Say
this morning that they thought he was prepared To dye as To fiting We
hant had nary battle sense the battle at Bethel Church  all of our men has
Gone down there know But our ridgment gineral Mcgrooder has tuck 10
thousand men down there    [Gen. John Bankhead Magruder] And is agoing
to attact newport news  this is The Morn ing that he was to Make the attact
But we hant herd from them to day  it will be asevear attact for they ar well
fortyfide there  I think our men will tak it But they will lose many of ther
men  they left here the other day with John and Brach hmhills [Hemphill's]
Brother he dyde here and they tuck him home  I want you to give John
hemphill houdy for me  tell him that I would be glad To Se him  tell old ant
Cate hemphill houdy for me I am so weake that I Cant hardley setup to Rite
But I will try to give you alittle histry of the battle At Manases Junction on
sunday the 20 of July they had apourful Battle there  they fit one hole day
they only kiled about 5 hundred of our men andwonded about 4 or 5
thousand  our men kiled 7 or 8 thousand of the yankes & wonded 15 or 18
thousand of them  We whipt them Badley and tuck every thing they had
the say when they did Retrete that they run over one another & women &
Children and kiled lots of them selves  I supose the like never was knowd in
the world  our men got about 70 peaces of Canon & 20 thousand stand of
armes And 500 wagons & teames besides thousands of other things  they
say what they got from the Enemy was worth one Million & ahalf of dollars
If I made no mistake in reding your letter I think that you said that mother
said if she had Somebody to Come with her that she would Come To se me
I would give this hold world if I Could Just se her Coming But that I never
expect to Se  tell My Dear old mother houdy for me  if I Could se her this

morning I dont know what I would give  I still try to pray that I may live to git home onst more to se you all But it is doutful about that  tell Mr Walker that I send him houdy and my best love & Respects  tell him to Remember me in all of his prays  give Mrs Satterwhite and famley houdy for me and all inquirn friends  tell Gorge & gemima houdy for me  tell them that I think they Might Rite to me  I would rite to them But I so mutch riting to do for our boys that I hant got the Chance  tell mr alen that I hant forgot what I ow him & if I live to git back I will pay him  give him my respects  olumbus & Joseph Williams is well  it mity Bad to be sick here for there Is nothing to eate that asick man Can eat  We ar looking for thomas walton & others here today  mary Rote to me that she was going to send me abox of Aples & Cucumbers & unions  she would send me Somthing that I Could eat But she hant the Money to git it with nor I Cant no money to send To her  We hant got no Cent of our wagers yet  they Ow us about [?] dollars each know if could some of it we Could by somthing that we Could eat here But it would be hye to pay ther prices  Afew lines to Marthy  it made proud to think that you put up your potisions in my behalf  Marthy I do hope and pray that they wer herd and ansurd in haven I also try to pray for you all as well as I know how  there is aheep of wekeedness going on here But thank God I never have have pertuck with none of it nor I never intend to as long as I live  let that be long or short  I want you to beshure to Rite sone as this Comes to hand If we should live to se that time Role Round  We will be disbanded the 13 of november in Raleigh So nothing more at present only Remanes your loving Brother till Death So farwell

Peter Poteet to F.M. Poteet
And famley Mother and all inquirnes friends

Burke County Collections

1. Isaac Avery letter to Laura Avery, 18 Oct 1862. Avery Family of North Carolina Papers, #33. Southern Historical Collection, Louis Round Wilson Library, University of North Carolina at Chapel Hill.

2. Col. Isaac Avery message to Isaac T. Avery, 2 July 1863. NC Digital Collections. State Archives of North Carolina: Vault Collection.

3. William W. Avery letter to Isaac T. Avery, 8 Jul 1863. Avery Family of North Carolina Papers, #33. Southern Historical Collection, Louis Round Wilson Library, University of North Carolina at Chapel Hill.

4. John A. McPherson letter to Gen. Isaac T. Avery, 3 Aug 1863. Folder 26, Avery Family of North Carolina Papers, #33. Southern Historical Collection, Louis Round Wilson Library, University of North Carolina at Chapel Hill.

5. Eliza M. Walton letter to Thomas G. Walton, 26 Dec 1861. Eliza Murphy Walton Letters, 1834; 1861-1863, #2686-z. Southern Historical Collection, Louis Round Wilson Library, University of North Carolina at Chapel Hill.

6. Thomas G. Walton letter to Eliza M. Walton, 2 May 1862. Eliza Murphy Walton Letters, 1834; 1861-1863, #2686-z. Southern Historical Collection, Louis Round Wilson Library, University of North Carolina at Chapel Hill.

7. Eliza M. Walton letter to John M. ("Jock") Walton , 25 July 1864. Thomas George Walton Papers, #748. Southern Historical Collection, Louis Round Wilson Library, University of North Carolina at Chapel Hill.

8. Thomas G. Walton letter to Eliza M. Walton, 16 Jan 1862. Personal property, descendants of the Walton Family, Morganton, NC.

9. Thomas G. Walton letter to Eliza M. Walton, 23 Jan 1862. Personal property, descendants of the Walton Family, Morganton, NC.

10. Thomas G. Walton letter to Eliza M. Walton, 2 Apr 1862. Personal property, descendants of the Walton Family, Morganton, NC.

11. Thomas G. Walton letter to Eliza M. Walton, 9 Apr 1862. Personal property, descendants of the Walton Family, Morganton, NC.

12. Peter Poteet letter to Francis M. Poteet, 16 Jul 1861. Poteet-Dickson Letters, 1861-1902. Hunter Library Digital Collections, Western Carolina University, Cullowhee, NC.

13. Peter Poteet letter to Francis M. Poteet, 7 Aug 1861. Poteet-Dickson Letters, 1861-1902. Hunter Library Digital Collections, Western Carolina University, Cullowhee, NC.

.

# 4. CALDWELL COUNTY COLLECTIONS

## Edmund Walter Jones Papers, 1789-1917

Private Walter Lenoir Jones was the son of Edmund Jones and Ann
Lenoir Jones of Happy Valley in Caldwell County. Walter attended
Hillsboro Military Academy in Orange County, NC, but few letters remain
of his experiences during the Civil War. Jones was killed at Gettysburg in
1863.

Walter's brother, Colonel John Thomas Jones was a student at the
University of North Carolina from 1860-1861. He served in the 1st NC
Volunteers and then as an officer in the 26th NC Regiment under Zebulon
B. Vance and in the brigade of James Johnston Pettigrew. He was killed in
May 1864 at the Battle of the Wilderness.

Walter and John Thomas Jones were grandsons of William Lenoir of
Happy Valley in Caldwell County.

## Lenoir Family Papers, 1763-1940, 1969-1975

William Lenoir, a general in the American Revolution and later a
North Carolina politician resided at his family home, Fort Defiance, in
Caldwell County. The Lenoir family had close ties to the Avery family in
Burke County since two of Lenoir's sons married Waightstill Avery's
daughters. William Lenoir's son and daughter-in-law, Thomas and Selina
Louisa Avery Lenoir, also lived at "Fort Defiance," and their son Walter
Waightstill Lenoir, a lawyer in Lenoir, is the subject of many of the letters
in this collection. Thomas and Selina Lenoir's son-in-law Joseph Caldwell
Norwood (J.C.), a teacher in Hillsborough, North Carolina, writes about
Stoneman's Raid.

## Chiliab Smith Howe Papers, 1814-1899

Laura Norwood, a niece of Walter W. Lenoir, wrote to her cousin
Ellen Richardson, granddaughter of Alabama governor Israel Pickens,
about her devotion to the cause of the Confederacy and state politics. Her
letter became part of the Chiliab Smith Howe C.ollection.

## Private Walter Jones to Edmund Jones[1]

Camp Bee Aquia Creek Aug 23 1861

Dear Father

I would have written to you before but the mails all so uncertain that it is doubtful that you would have got it or not. There is no certain regular mail to this place. We are all well and in fine spirits and are spoiling for a fight. We are stationed about three miles from the Potomac river and some of our batteries firing at the Yankee vessels every day or two when they venture too far. We have the North Point gun which was taken at Manassas. They threw two shells on board the Pawnee with her yesterday and killed several. We are about fifteen thousand strong here under the command of General Holmes of North Carolina. I saw him today and he is a very hard looking case it would make the Yankees men [afraid] to look at him. We were inspected by him this morning and he sayed our was a very fine company indeed. We had also another compliment paid us the other day by the Col of the Second Georgia regiment. He sayed ours was the best drilled company in the skirmish drill he had ever seen. We drill it entirely by the bugle. When we left Richmond we expected to be in a fight before night and we heard they were fighting at that time at the mouth of this creek and you may imagine how badly we were disapointed when we arrived to hear that there had been but a few shots fired at the vessels. I have no idea how long we will stay here or anything about the movements of the troops as we have not seen a paper since I got here. We are encamped in a beautiful place on the top a young mountain and can see the river and the yankees too sometimes that is their vessels.

We are off about a mile from any other regiment and it is found to be a healthy place although there is a good deal of sickness moving through the troops on account of the marshes but there is not other kind of sickness as I know of. There are five North Carolina regiments at this place. Col. Tew and Col. Stokes among the number. We live pretty hard now. I tell you we have not had a mouthful of bacon in two weeks but live entirely on fresh beef without salt as we cannot get it any where but will weigh nearly 175 pounds and every man in the company looks better than they did when we left home. If you do not hear from me as often as you expect you must not imagine there is any thing the matter with me as it is very seldom we can get the chance to send letters off from here.

How are all of the friends in the Valley and your own health and little

Marys? I think of her fifty times a day and would give any thing to see her. Kiss her for me and tell her she must not forget brother Wat. Give my love to Will and Mary and tell them I would like to hear from them and know how they are navigating. I suppose they stay at Clover Hill most of the time. I hear that Coot has got entirely well. Give him my love and tell him he must make haste and get big enough to fight the Yankees. Also give my love to aunt Connie and uncle Finley and all of the rest who ask about me. Send love to all.

Your affectionate Son

Wat

PS Write soon and direct to Richmond VA Care Col. Pettigrew Co A 12th Reg N.C. Vols.

## J.T. [John Thomas] Jones to Edmund Jones[2]

Camp ___hall
April 26th/64

Dear Father,

I have just received your letter by Holden and was very much surprised to hear that you had not but one letter from me since my return. I have written at least five letters if not more. I sent you photographs in two which I hope you have gotten.

I hardly know what to think of our friends movements in this quarter. It is generally thought here now that Grant has received no material reinforcements. Whether under the circumstances or not, he will advance somewhere soon. It may be on the Peninsula only to hold us here. I had a long conversation with Gen Lee, a day or two ago since. He is in the highest of spirits and seems to think our prospects here never been so in Virginia. He says other movements of importance are on foot in North Carolina. I hope they may succeed. If we are only successful in this campaign I believe will find us all at home. We should certainly advance soon if Grant does not. We have sent all of our tents and waggons to the rear and are ready to march or remain until Longstreet's command has not arrived down toward Fredericksburg and a greater part of the Calvary has. The Burnside expedition is the one we have most to fear from. I think it is intending to advance by the peninsula and will more with a rapidity when it starts. I hope we will be ready for him. Our Army certainly has never in so fine a condition and they feel confident of our success. I think you need not fear that we will be able to hold out on account of provisions. You people do not know how little your son lived upon. I find a splendid dinner today of cornbread and a slice of pork. Yesterday I had only bread. I got the books you sent me by Lt. Sudderth, they suit me very well. You spoke to me in your last letter on the subject of religion. I can tell you this much, I often think seriously of such things and think I would be confirmed if an opportunity should happen. I thought of speaking to Annie on the subject when I was home but had no chance.

I am glad that Judge Reed spent a few days with you.I think such company helps you from being lonely and I hear you will grow rather [?]. Do you not think there is a danger of it. I am surprised that you have not found some excuse to visit Greensboro. We have just seen a short piece of Gov'r Vance's speech at Fayetteville and I must say a great many of his friends in the army are not pleased by its tone. They think he is rather backing down. What do you think of it?

Did you see that letter of mine in the Enquirer to Col Burgwyn? I was surprised at this being published as I never had any idea he would. He wrote to me saying he intended writing a piece to defend Pettigrew's brigade and asking me to give him a short sketch of the 3rd Days fight at Gettysburg which I did thinking he just wanted a few points from which to write his article. It was written in a great hurry just as we got back to Culpepper and then once one or two slight misunderstandings. My love to aunt and all her children.

Your aff son
JT Jones

## Walter Lenoir to Thomas I. Lenoir[3]

Thos. I. Lenoir

Tucker's Barn Feby 11th 1863

Dear Brother

I wrote to you about two weeks ago from Marion, where I had gone with Mr. Montgomery to examine Mr. Wakefield's artificial leg. I went with him last week to Statesville to examine Mr. Stockton's leg. Mr. Stockton uses the leg made by Palmer of Philadelphia which I believe has more reputation than any other used in this country. Wakefield's was made by Ord. of Phil. The machinery of both seemed to be on the same principal, except that Stockton, having a very short stump, walked on his knee, with the stump, hardly an inch long, folded back. Wakefield's had a ring into which the stump was inserted, so as to catch the weight at the swell of the leg bones just below the joint. The weight can not be rested on the end of the stump as that always remains tender. I find myself disappointed upon inquiring as the the efficiency of the artificial legs, and will have to make up my mind to be a worse cripple than I had hoped for. I have not been to the Fort since my return form Statesville, being blockaded by the snow, which fell here about ten inches deep. It is melting rapidly now, but is still abundant. I was quite helpless when it was at the worst, and couldn't help feeling discouraged about Haywood. Montgomery has done but little towards my leg (which will be like Mr. Wakefield's) and as it will be rather a tedious job my coming to Haywood seems to be a good ways off. We are all as well as usual here, except that I am suffering some with tooth ache which by the by is a poor companion for a letter writer, and entitles me to some allowance for such a careless and scattering letter. I will get Rufus to cut the graft for which you wrote when I go over to the Fort, which I expect to do as soon as the roads are passable. Your letters have been irregular and slow in coming in, but I suppose most, perhaps all of them arrive in the course of time. The mail still leaves Morganton for Lenoir and the Fort on Tuesday in time to get to Lenoir by night. Letters arriving in Morganton after Tuesday would still come with little delay by way of Hickory Station if the P.M.'s do their duty. They have a daily mail from Morganton to Hickory station and a tri-weekly mail from that point to Lenoir.

I am sorry to hear that [?] has done so badly about vacating the house, and that he had the misfortune to lose his own by his delay in occupying it. If you had such a snow as we have had, I suppose that will fix him some longer. I hope you will try to make Andy and his family earn their board, and that they will get along so as not to be very troublesome. I have thought often of the burden they would be to you if you should have much sickness among your negro family. Sister Laura sends her love. Laura says that [L?] will answer Lizzie's letter in a few days. My general health continues good, but I begin to suffer for the want of exercise, and have ceased to fatten for some time past. I avoid walking on my knee, as it tends to crook the joint. When I get my new leg I hope I can go enough to keep me in health. Give my love to sister Lizzie.

Your affectionate brother Walter

## Laura Norwood to Walter W. Lenoir[4]

Lenoir July 20th 1863

My dear Uncle Walt,

Pa wanted to write to you and uncle John both this evening but inasmuch as I thought it doubtful any way whether he would accomplish both letters, and I wished very much to write, I have claimed the privilege of so doing. Your very welcome letter was received a week ago and I have been <u>on my head</u> to answer it ever since for I had a lot of things to tell you, but I waited for news from Tom, and now I have heard <u>that</u>, all the other things are swallowed up, clear gone, and done forgot forever more!

Well, bless Tom's old soul! He is a great old boy, now ain't he! He is safe _ Tom is, we heard it today after a lingering suspense of more than two weeks, a suspense that was becoming painful in the extreme and fast setting into a conviction of some heavy misfortune. Only think we heard from all our friends one after another and even Hose Stallings wrote home to his father, and still not a word from Tom, and Uncle William would write and say he could not hear. But this morning after we had started Jim to Wilkesboro to see if Mrs. Col. B knew anything, we got a letter from Tom himself!

Safe at Uncle Williams in Richmond, wounded in the left shoulder, but not severely and doing first rate! His adventures have been romantic and creditable in a high degree. How I would like to be Tom! But before I proceed and relate Tom's adventures I must tell you the fate of the rest of our friends.

Cousin Isaac Avery is dead – He was buried at Williamsport, John Jones came through unhurt and such was the dreadful mortality in Pettigrew's Brigade that John is now the ranking officer of the whole Brigade and it is at present under his command. He is colonel of the 26th Col. Burgwyn and Lt Col. Lane both killed. Gen. Pettigrew died of wounds on the 17th inst. – being at the time in command of the division. Walter L. Jones was badly wounded in the thigh and arm and left at Gettysburg. His thigh was broken near the body. – Uncle William thinks from Tom's acct that he cannot recover. Col Barber is safe. Tom does not mention anybody else in the 27th except poor Will Mickle who was killed. He was struck at the same time that Tom was, was very near him, He uttered one cry and fell motionless and did not move afterwards. Tom thinks that is no doubt of his death, but

I still have a faint hope.

Our companies from this county which were in 26th were terribly cut up. 20 or more, in all, killed, and nearly all the rest slightly wounded, not many seriously. Loyd Jones and Phillip Largent are the only ones in Co. F that escaped unhurt. This was Rankin's old company. I send you Tuttles report also some honorable mention of 26th. Cousin Nolton and Willoughby Avery escaped unhurt. Cousin William Norwood (Georgetown) slightly wounded, Also, Thomas Hill Norwood, John Tillinghast, Johnny Norwood (Georgetown) all unhurt. Robert Bingham, captured at South Anna Bridge and sent to Fort Warren. Will Norwood from Savannah in very bad health and discharged. Dr. John and Heywood not heard from. Co. A 22nd lost two men. Killed, McMillan and Keller. Cousin Ed cannot do anything for Walter. Citizens not allowed to go further than Winchester. We are all well here and at Fort – in usual health, that is. We have very nice time indeed – Cousin Rebecca is absolutely a fortune for any body for a daughter sister, wife, or any thing. I would like so much to be Cousin Rebecca! But if I was Tom – as I said before, I would hardly be Rebecca, but, she is splendid. Uncle William is delighted at Tom's escape, etc. I have concluded to copy Tom's letter and send it to you as it seemed to have such a happy effect on the rest of us, especially Helen and me, who had a mind to retreat to the woods and first holler our very raving best till our emotions subsided. Mamie cried, Pa came in one of it, – Jule was hardly afterwards found in the top of a high tree, I guess it was the effect of the letter that send her up. Ma looked up and merely said "Julia! Come down" – "Well, Ma'm" sung out Julia from mid air and every body was so glad to notice it.

We all send our love. I am going to be mighty good about writing to you. I don't see how your books were ever appreciated as much before or ever treated with such marked consideration. I wish you were here. You must come and our dear love to all. Crops rather damaged by rain. Mr. Evans is here and speak of taking more land and some forms – Pa will write Col Peter Evans in Washington City at a friend house badly wounded.

With much love
Yours

Laura N-

P. S. Can't think Haywood is much in the world. Must be hanging over the edge if not entirely out.

**General William Lenoir**

## Walter W. Lenoir to His Brother[5]

Crab Orchard, July 23rd, 1863

Dear Brother,

A shower of rain has made me hobble from the cornfield; to which I sometimes venture for a while, though to but little purpose; and I have set down to scratch you a line. It continues very wet, and I like the rest of farmers have a poor chance to work. My forward corn is beginning to tassle, and I will have to lay some of it by with the third working. I have made myself a leg which I am beginning to use in walking about the farm. I hope I will be able to use it for walking without discontinuing the use of the Montgomery leg for riding and an occasional change.

After writing to you last week as to the course which I thought our army ought to pursue as to private property in Pennsylvania, I received in the papers Gen. Lee's orders to his army on the subject. I hope you have seen them and read them. They breathe the spirit of a noble hearted christian soldier and have raised that great man still higher in my estimation than he stood before. And the good conduct of our army towards the people of Pennsylvania, (to which there were necessarily but too many exceptions,) has raised it and the South still higher in my love and admiration than they stood before; and will shine out forever in bright contrast with the infamous conduct of our enemies. Gen. Jenkins, whose command the Yankees themselves are forced to compliment for the gentlemanly behavior, has a fine dwelling house in western Va. the parlor of which the Yankees have for a long time used for a cavalry stable, and many of his troopers are his neighbors who have been used in the like manner. Retaliation in kind would have done us no good. His mode of retaliation has gained a great and substantial advantage.

The course of events and my reflections of late have led me to modify my opinions as to some of the darker and more horrid aspects of the war, growing out of the subject of slavery. You know that I have never regarded Lincoln's Proclamation as making of itself much substantial difference in the conduct of the war. The Yankees have gone on since doing just what they were doing before, and in the same manner, so far as the slaves and slavery is concerned.

You know too that I have not dreaded their attempts to arm the slaves, believing that their presence in their armies would be a cause of weakness instead of strength, and that they would be shrewd enough to know that or soon find it out, and limit the experiment to such bounds as they thought it would be sufficient to keep the South in a state of alarm. I did think, however, that to the extent that they were introduced, it would make the war more horrid, because I supposed that our men would refuse to capture them when found fighting, as well as the white officers who commanded them. In this I find I was mistaken. Our troops capture negro soldiers and their officers and treat them as they do the others. And this I have no doubt now will continue to be the case to the end of the war. I still think, for the reasons that I have already mentioned, that there will be but little use made by the Yankees of their negro soldiers, though I see that Gen. Banks tries to make them out quite valiant. It is so natural to man to fight that it is possible that even the negro diciplined and led by white men may stand fire better than we of the South have supposed. But even if this is so, amalgamation in the ranks with them as well as every where else is so very unnatural that not even Yankees fanaticism will fail in the attempt. That, however, is not the point which I set out to state, which was merely that the addition of negro troops to the Yankee army would not as I now think prevent them from being taken prisoners by our troops when in their power, as their mean white associates now are.

My views have undergone a still greater change on another and much more important point in this connexion. I have as you know never thought that the Yankees would succeed in liberating our slaves. I believe that God over rules the affairs of nations, and that He will not suffer the Yankees to perpetrate so great a crime as that against us and their species. But while we know that His ways are not as our ways, and are past finding out, and often seem very mysterious to our imperfect perceptions. We are not certain therefore beyond a doubt but that it may be his righteous will that our enemies may succeed in this. Looking at the possibility of such a thing, and considering it in the light of human reason and experience, I took it almost for granted at first that such a forcible emancipation would lead to scenes of horrid massacre and butchery; that the negroes finding freedom in their grasp, and having their passions inflamed by the fierce teachings of abolitionist would attempt to slay their masters, and that they in turn would be compelled to destroy the negroes. This was the view commonly taken of the matter at the South, and no doubt still is; and with the history of Hayti before their eyes and the knowledge that it was such men as Lane and Lovejoy and such books as Helper's impending crisis that has brought the Yankees to attempt such a thing, it was very natural that such should have been the feeling of the South. But I now believe that if the Yankees succeed in subjugating the white people of the South and freeing the negroes it will be without any massacres except such as are now taking place upon the battle field. There will be no rising upon the non-combatant men, women or children. Those of us who choose to see it will see their Yankee masters set the negroes free and then govern them and their fellow citizens, their late masters and mistresses, as well as the people of subjugated are governed by other enlightened nations. Bad as the Yankees are they would not wish the whites of the South to be massacred by the negroes and would not permit it. You may wonder why my views have changed in this respect. Partly by reflection, partly by the light of facts. The Yankees have for the present at least actually freed the slaves in a large part of the South, and in portions where they were in the greatest numbers, and had had the worst treatment on the sugar plantations in La. for instance. Yet it has led to no massacre and there is less probability that it would lead to it if they were entirely successful in their attempt. What that mercenary and speculating people expect to make by reducing us to the condition of Jamaica is a great mystery to me. But if they succeed I have no doubt that it will be done as peaceably, so far as collision between the two races is concerned as it was done in Jamaica. If the Yankees are strong enough to put down their fierce and strong fight for independence they will be strong enough to govern the negroes afterwards, and I have little doubt for my part that if the South is subdued by the North it will be as well governed and prosperous as Jamaica. Not a very tempting prospect truly, not one that I would expect to remain to witness if I could pay or beg my way to some other country. I have drawn this gloomy picture, not for the purpose of adding it to the many gloomy ones that already darken your mind, but in order to rid it, if I can, as I have done my own of the still gloomier one of assassination and general massacre, which being the worst possible result of the entire success of the Yankees is I fear the one which your mind is too prone at times to fasten upon in the exclusion of every other. Nor do I write such things because I have any greatly increased apprehensions that we will fail in establishing our independence. I am by no means disheartened by the loss of Vicksburg and Port Hudson. They held out so well that I began to hope they would be received by Johnson, cholera and yellow fever. But who would have anticipated after the comparative easy fall of New Orleans and Memphis that they would have resisted so long the gigantic efforts that have been made to them? Our next position will be away from the water, and if Lincoln is as long in reducing it he will have to hand over the job unfinished to his successor. We still hold Charleston, Wilmington and Mobile and Savannah it is true, all upon the water, at least we still hold them all according to my last news. But if they were reduced, and it would take time to reduce them all, if we may judge the future by the past, we would still have an army that Lincoln could not reduce before his democratic congress meets. The peace party which seems to be growing rapidly now as the North will begin to conclude that the war is 'played out'.

You know I thought last winter we would have more and harder fighting this year than any before, and that there would not be much afterwords. I still think so.

We are very anxious about Tom Norwood and many other friends who were in the battle of Gettysburg. I have not seen a word about the 37th. We saw it stated that Col. Avery was killed but see no confirmation of it since, and hope it is not so. Please write to me about the Averys and tell me what you can about the casualties in the Caldwell companies. I have written you a much longer letter than I intended, and am not through yet. I wrote to cous. Will Lenoir of Ten. and got an answer telling who of his nephews are in the service which I must write about next time. Love to all.

Your brother

## Walter W. Lenoir to Selina L. Lenoir[6]

Crab Orchard Jany 15th 1864

Dear Mother

I have been rather negligent of late about writing letters, for a reason for a reason that should perhaps have made me write the oftener, the irregularity of the mails. There has been no snow here yet; but for all that we are having they say a colder winter than usual. I have not yet quite finished the cabin for my negroes which has been so much in the way of my other work. The boys are now at work upon the chimney which they are making of stone, and I think are succeeding pretty well for their first attempt. It will be quite a comfortable cabin for them when finished, and I hope to see them at length moved into it some day next week. My farming operatives make but a poor figure, owing to the destructive frost in September. I am short of every thing except rough food for my stock, of which I have enough, perhaps some to spare. My corn and other grain ought to do me very well till harvest, after paying my tithes. I made 1400 lbs of pork which is not enough for my folks for a year, at the rate they have been consuming bacon since I came out. If the corn fed to the hogs had not been seriously impaired by the frost, I would have had some bacon to spare after paying my tithe. Maria and Delia have done very badly about spinning, not having spun filling enough during the year to make comfortable allowances for clothing for the negroes. Maria has not worked out a day, Delia only in the corn crop, and a few other days in the hay and oat harvest, and Clarissa none for about two months, besides helping some times during crop time, about washing etc.

I have had a poor chance to regulate them and have not attempted it, but if the Yankees are not kind enough to take them off my hands, they will have to make a great change soon, or have another master. I find upon trial so far that I can manage the man and boys with more comfort than I expected; but though I always considered the negroes a pest, mine are dirtier and lazier than even I counted on. It is true that I am a good deal to blame for it myself, as I have not attempted yet to control them; but I find that if I am to get along with them at all, I must nerve myself to the very disagreeable task of instituting and keeping up strict discipline over them. I have been postponing, and feel still like postponing what I know will be a hard piece of work, in the hope that circumstances would soon make it more clear to my mind whether I would be willing and able to keep them. Maria has not been doing very well since the birth of her last child and seems to be threatened with something like falling of the womb. She seems to be getting better now and I hope will escape from so serious a calamity  Except that she and all my negroes have so far been blessed with remarkably good health.

The Yankees have made no demonstration in this direction yet; but I fear we will not escape them when warm weather comes. Our best protections will be our poverty and bad roads, which will make it cheaper for them to buy their grain and beef in the North West than steal them here. There is no probability of their coming here except on raids for supplies, as long as we maintain any large armies in the field.

Tom's and Lizzie's heath about as usual. My own continues very good. I send my love to all the family including cousin Julia. Some of the folks at the fort or the Barn might write to us oftener than they have been doing of late.

I remain Dear Mother

Your affectionate Son

W W Lenoir

## J.C. Norwood to Walter W. Lenoir[7]

Lenoir 2d Apl. 1865

Dear Walter

We are just through with a scene of alarm & very great danger. Stoneman has just swept through the country with 10,000 cavalry towards Wilkesboro, Salem, Salisbury Greensboro Hillsboro & Raleigh — & we fear there will be no adequate preparation made to meet him. About dark on Tuesday evening last the heart of the column reached the Factory & in a few minutes the people around were under guard & the command in camp! They were equipped in the very best manner, & under the severest discipline & were not allowed to plunder to any great extent or commit any acts of violence. They left about 3 O'clock next day Wednesday (29th) except 2 companies that were left to burn the Factory — which they did with great coolness and method. They also set fire to the storehouse & grainery &c. Most of the store-house the cotton house Tanery [sic] & oil [unclear] escaped. The little office joining the store was burned — the last of them left by sundown. They reached Wilkesboro next evening about dark taking it by surprise also — we hear that Just. Findley's house was burned — but hope it is a mistake — many of them said that a large body of infantry was behind — we suppose has gone towards Virginia. So complete was their guard that they were all taken by surprise down the river & lost all of their horses and mules except Genl Patterson's one little pony which they couldn't catch & Rufus one which happens to be out of the way. I have not seen Rufus being afraid to leave home — A soldier who was there upon their arrival & made his escape gave us the facts about 2 O'clock that night — And went on to the station. We did all we could in the way of hiding necessaries & running off negroes & stock but none of them came home. While at the Factory they made cousin Rufus' room their head quarters & treated him courteously — behaved very [seedily] at Cousin Ed's the Fort & other places — but committed no violence. They told cousin Rufus that the secessionists down the river would fare badly. We suppose that their next stop would be Elkin or [Janesboro]. The force which passed the Factory — six thousand was commanded by Guilam. Stoneman joined him at Holoman's Ford with 4 thousand. It is said a third column passed through Jefferson & camped over the river from Wilkesboro. I hope that is not so. About two days before a considerable number of negro men left for Tennessee — & have not been heard from since including 4 from the Fort. 1 Genl. Patterson's 12 E. Jones & 5 from here. Elias John Turner Jones and Wash — from the fort-Larkin Erin Jerry & Joe — I have not heard to[o many] went with the cavalry. Some of the officers cursed the negroes &

wished them all in Hell. We had been for some time before under constant apprehension about tory or robber raids & I have been serving on guard at town every third night & have been as much as two weeks with out taking off my clothes. We are always in danger except when a portion of Avery's command is here which is not very often — Home guard no account. A few days before these troubles commenced I rec. your War_Song & other [piece] we were all very much pleased with them especially the song of which I had the girls to make a good many copies & distribute it pretty generally — & I was about to send it to 3 of the papers — but will wait now until the Storm is passed.

Yours affecty
JC Norwood

The girls will write more in detail

## Laura Norwood to Ellen Richardson[8]

Lenoir. Feb 28th. 1862.

My dear Ellen,

This is fast day but Nature seems have put on a festival dress. All out of doors is so bright, sunshiny and gay. I am a little afraid that hungriness is very much conducive to despondency when there is no prospect of satisfying the appetite, but although I am feeling the want of food very sensibly just at present, and have been listening for two hours, I mean one hour, was <u>at</u> <u>church</u> two, to Mr. Rankin, the Presbyterian Minister who is dry as a last years cornstalk. Still, I hope nothing like a desponding tone will pervade this letter. If it does, my darling, ascribe it to physical and not mental causes, to the want of dinner but not the absence of devotion to the Cause of our Country, — dearer, far dearer in the hour of its peril than in the day of its many victories. I would here state, before I get any <u>hungrier</u>, that I am in <u>no</u> <u>sense</u> defeated because Buckner, Pillow, Floyd, or whoever it is, is defeated. No Indeed! The Yankees did not capture my spirit of Resistance when they took Donelson. Nashville seems to have suddenly become a fabulous place, a place today in Lincolndom and tomorrow in the Confederacy, and Pillow, Buckner, & Floyd & Johnson flit about in the telegrams from one place to another and from one state of being to another. We cannot get any certain information about them here, but be it as bad as it may be, I am not conquered or bewildered. Who ever expected that we would gain our independence without a desperate struggle? I certainly did not. And I think if it were gained by a succession of brilliant victories, it would not long abide. A people untried by adversity are unfit to be the founders of a great nation. But Ellen dear it is of no use for me to write on these subjects to you, for no idea on these questions exists in my mind, that has not probably occured to yours, and I could not find expressions more clear or forcible than those which will naturally present themselves to you. One thing which pleases me very much and I think shows a spirit of earnestness in the people, is the way in which the fast days appointed by our good president are observed. Today, the church was crowded, and the militia officers, who were drilling in town, all filed in and took their places, and the whole congregation seemed attentive and solemn. The sermon was very good, forcible and sensible, though somewhat less effective than it might have been if some one else had preached it.

Tomorrow there will be a dinner in honor of the volunteers who belong to our first company: they have re-enlisted and are at home on furlough. Pa, and some other gentlemen will address them. Several new companies are in process of being formed in this county, and those in the field will probably re-enlist at least a large majority. Brother Tom will join the army in a few weeks. Cousin Ed Jones came home last week from the convention at Raleigh. He is very blue over the state of affairs. In fact I am afraid the men who are at the head of the State Government are for the most part very inefficient and stupid. Roanoke Island is a name that is not at all suggestive of pleasant things. I suppose our men did right to surrender, but from what I hear, they did not win much renown in the little fighting they did do. Capt. Wise's company certainly acted with great gallantry; but I have not heard yet of any other company that did.

Our Gov. Clarke is a very ordinary man; our Adjutant Genl. is certainly a very "sorry" man; and I am afraid our convention dont know what ought to be done. In fact, the people of the Old North bid fair to be badly represented by her rulers. But as to the Mountain region, there is no portion of the Confederacy more firmly and enthusiastically devoted to our cause. The counties that border on East Tennessee are sound and loyal. There was a little boy from Watauga here the night we heard of the Donelson defeat, and he sprang up and said "If the Yankees <u>do</u> come into this country, I am <u>one</u> that they will have to <u>drop</u> in their path." His neighborhood has been threatened with invasion from East Tenn., and he said this in prospect of real danger. The Wautagians are the finest looking soldiers I have seen. They make our house their stopping place on the way to the Station. Nine staid here a few nights ago. Some times six or seven walk in, just as we are sitting down to dinner, which causes a little cloud to arise on the face of our fair housekeeper, my sister Mary. We have laughed at Mama a good deal about the Volunteers. Most of them belong to the 37th N.C. Regiment which contains many of my friends and acquaintances, and I very often ask after the officers and others that I think they will be sure to know. Mama said one day "Laura is such a coquette, dont you see how she <u>carries on</u> with the soldiers"? The idea was so absurd that it seemed a very witty remark. Poor Me! So hopelessly sensible, and positive, I never knew the delights of a fliration. Never will <u>now</u>, for I am indisputably "not girlish any more". Well "act well our part, there all the honor lies". If my part is that of an old maid, I accept it without fear for I never feared any thing, and it is a poor time to begin the business now. I am often glad I am <u>not</u> married, but methinks there is some thing very fine in having a brave husband to fight in the glorious battles, and come home and tell about them by the fireside. I declare it would be fine to <u>own</u> such a brave officer as — , Well I wont say who. He is a splendid looking man, as bold and brave as any Knight of the olden time, and therefore worthy of a more beautiful ladye love than myself who care nothing for him any way, nor he for me. Only it would be quite fine, and patriotic to say "My Husband Maj." — There! There are some volunteers now at the door! I must leave here. They must come to the fire. I will go in Ma's room, that refuge for the exile. My dear, did you ever live in a crowded house? If you never did, you will never know how to sympathise with Noah's weary dove that soared the earth around &c.

Sometimes at night, I go from one fireside to another, from the parlor to the sitting-room & thence to Ma's room, and thence upstairs before I find a resting place. There are various comfortable little <u>colonies</u> in different parts of the house this evening.

Ma joins me in love to all, especially Cousin Julia. We have not heard any thing from our Tennessee kin for a month or two. They are Southerners. Some of the younger ones in the army. What is the No. of your husbands Regt. and who commands it? I always look anxiously when I see any thing said about Mississippi troops. Dearest excuse this, the boys and girls are talking around me in the most inexcusable manner. Poor Cousin Sarah is rapidly declining. All the others well. I am so sorry for poor Laura. I love her very much. Write soon to

Laura.

## Caldwell County Collections

1. Walter Jones letter to Edmund Jones, 23 Aug 1861. Folder 10, Edmund Walter Jones Papers, #3543. Southern Historical Collection, Louis Round Wilson Library, University of North Carolina at Chapel Hill.

2. John T. Jones letter to Edmund Jones, 26 Apr 1864. Folder 12, Edmund Walter Jones Papers, #3543. Southern Historical Collection, Louis Round Wilson Library, University of North Carolina at Chapel Hill.

3. Walter W. Lenoir letter to Thomas I. Lenoir, 11 Feb 1863. Folder 151, Lenoir Family Papers, #426. Southern Historical Collection, Louis Round Wilson Library, University of North Carolina at Chapel Hill.

4. Laura Norwood letter to Walter W. Lenoir, 20 Jul 1863. Folder 152, Lenoir Family Papers, #426. Southern Historical Collection, Louis Round Wilson Library, University of North Carolina at Chapel Hill.

5. Walter W. Lenoir letter to Brother, 23 Jul 1863. Folder 152, Lenoir Family Paper,s #426. Southern Historical Collection, Louis Round Wilson Library, University of North Carolina at Chapel Hill.

6. Walter W. Lenoir letter to Selina L. Lenoir, 15 Jan 1864. Folder 154, Lenoir Family Paper,s #426. Southern Historical Collection, Louis Round Wilson Library, University of North Carolina at Chapel Hill.

7. J.C. Norwood letter to Walter W. Lenoir, 2 Apr 1865. Folder 156, Lenoir Family Papers, #426. Southern Historical Collection, Louis Round Wilson Library, University of North Carolina at Chapel Hill.

8. Laura Norwood letter to Ellen Richardson, 28 Feb 1862. Chiliab Smith Howe Papers, #3092. Southern Historical Collection, Louis Wilson Round Library, University of North Carolina at Chapel Hill.

# 5. HAYWOOD COUNTY COLLECTIONS

## Joseph Cathey and Cathey Family Papers

Joseph Cathey (1803-1874) was the son of William Cathey and Catherine Turner, some of the earliest settlers in Haywood County. Joseph Cathey was a farmer, a merchant and a miller in his community. He represented Haywood County at the North Carolina Constitutional Convention of 1835, and he served one term in the North Carolina Senate in 1842. Though he never served in the military, the title "Colonel" was bestowed upon him as a sign of respect for his position in the community. Cathey's wife was Nancy Hyatt, (1807-c.1850). A son, Capt. James M. Cathey, was killed at Petersburg, Virginia, in July 1864 while serving with the 25th NC Infantry, Company F. Another son, Lieut. Joseph Turner Cathey died in September 1863.

Additional papers of Joseph Cathey may be found in the Southern Historical Collection, Louis Round Wilson Library at the University of North Carolina at Chapel Hill. These papers are known as the Joseph Cathey Papers, 1833-1890.

## William H. Thomas Papers: Wartime North Carolina Collection

William Holland Thomas was the only white man ever to serve as the Principal Chief of the Eastern Band of Cherokee Indians. A colonel in the Confederate army, his famous "Thomas Legion" of western North Carolina and eastern Tennessee was composed of white and Native American soldiers. Thomas trained as an attorney and served as a North Carolina State Senator from 1848-1860. He owned stores in Haywood and Cherokee counties, worked as a trader among the Cherokees, and administered Indian affairs after the Civil War.

## J. Cathey to Rev. L.F. Siler[1]

Hominy Creek N.C.
Feb. 22rd 1861


Rev. L.F. Siler

Dear sir

      In the last No. of your paper I see published the proceedings of a meeting held at Waynesville on the 8th inst. as communicated to you In which I am made to say that I was in favor of N.C. sesceding with a view to reconstruction &c.

      I did say I was identified with the South as stated in the communication, and I further said that N.C. would not have her convention in session until after Lincoln would be in office, and would have indicated his policy, which if it should be to Carry out the Chicago platform, and we should fail to get an ajustment on the Crittenden plan, or the Virginia plan, or otherwise, then I thought Virginia and all the Border slave states would go out of the union, and I would then be for N.C. going out as stated in the Communication you published. --

      Now I will not say I have used the precise language here that I did on that ocasion, as I spoke without notes; and I now write by memory, but this I do know that these are the sentiments that I then intended to convey, and that I now hold. You will please give this a place in your paper at your erlyest convienance so that I may be set right before the public. and [?] may go

yours Very Truly

J. Cathey

p.s. papers copying the proceding of the meeting refered to above, will please copy this also. J.C.

### James W. Killian to Col. J. Cathey[2]

Davidson River
Jan 19 1863

[?] Cathey

Dear Sir

I arrived home last Friday Evening from the army near Fredricksburg  I found our mountain Boys general well and in fine Spirits and better clad than I expected to See them Gen Ransom & Gen Cooks Brigagis left there camps on the 4th Jan at 6 o clock a m for part unknown to them at the time while I was at Richmond they marched through the city  I went with them out 3 miles the night I was in Petirsburg they were in 2 miles of the city But did not see them  I understood they were a waiting for orders where to go  I seen Doct Fletcher at Raleigh  he told me there were ordered to Goldsboro NC and to the Rail Road was making arrangements to transport them from Petersburg to Goldsboro  If any other troops have been ordered from Gen Lees army I did not here it Capt James Cathey and a good many of his Boys sent a good large pack of money to your care and requested you to send an agent after it for them  I have directions in my possession  how you are to dispose of it  which directions I was to deliver to the agents who came after the money  my girls says send your Daughter Sarah I could tell you more about the Boys if I could see you more than I can write this morning

Very Truly yours
J.W. Killian

## Emma A. Shoolbred to Col. Cathey[3]

Flat Rock
March 30th 1863

Col. Cathey

Sir,

Though personally a stranger to you, I know that you are acquainted with my son James, and am induced to apply to you in a time of difficulty  I have been a widow for three years, and James and his two younger brothers being in the army, in Virginia, and my eldest at [?], I am entirely with out any one to assist me the war has greatly reduced my circumstances, and I find it hard to live.  I have many small negro children besides their parents to feed, and would be glad to know if I can purchase some corn from you at a reasonable price, and if you would allow me to purchase from you an ox, as I have lately lost one of mine, and understand from W. [?] Tabor that I cannot procure one in this neighborhood.  I should also be glad to know the price of wheat flour, and if I can get any from you. An early answer will oblige

yours respectfully,
E.A. Shoolbred

Flat Rock, N.C.
Please name the price of the ox corn and flour if I can obtain them from you or in your neighborhood.

Emma A. Shoolbred

## James B. Rankin to Col. J. Cathey[4]

Pleasant Gardens
August 11th 1863

Col J. Cathey

Dear Sir,

I see that you have been appointed a Director on the W.N.C. Rail Road, and I beg leave to address you in behalf of a friend of mine, whose name will be before the Board at your next meeting for an important office. It has, I believe, been reduced almost to a certainty that the present Chief Engineer will be turned out and if so another one will of course be[?]elect. I wish to urge upon you the claims of Maj. James W. Wilson for the office, if it should be made vacant. You may know Maj. Wilson, as he was for a time on this survey. He is in every way competent, being a capital Engineer, highly energetic and very [?] and skillful in the transaction and management of business matters, and further is deeply interested in the success of the road. It is the wish of Gov Vance that he should be elected, and I know that some of the most influential members of the Board are strongly in favour of him. I have no doubt that the change would be greatly to the interest of the Road. I write to you without Maj. Wilson's knowledge as he is at present in the army of Virginia. I do not write to you for the purpose of electioneering in the common acceptation [?] of the times, as I know you are a man fully capable of forming your own opionions in matters of this sort, but for the purpose of bringing the matter clearly before you, and of testifying to May. Wilson's competency and ability fully to discharge the duties of the office; and further I feared you might give some promise of support to some other applicant, though I do not know that there be any others. I suppose of course you will attend upon the next meeting of the Board, and if the matter should come up, which I have no doubt it will, I shall esteem it, not only a favour to Maj Wilson, but as I feel a great interest in the matter, I shall esteem it a favour personal to myself if you will give him your support.

Very truly your friend
James B. Rankin

## Nathaniel G. Phillips to Col. Cathey[5]

Valley Town, NC
Dec 24 1863

Col Cathey

sir the condition of this county renders it untenable the yankies and
Bushwhackers have Ruined it, & I will have to move my family out & as I
will soon have to Return to the army I want to move them in to your
county & my Father is a good miller & if you have a good mill he will take
it, & he can bring as good a Recommendation as you may desire. I want a
house & 8 or ten acres of land for my family & my father & mother want to
[?] go with me I hope you will try to help me I have been in the Service
nearly three years & my family has not got provisions to Do them a month
& the frost & the Bushwhackers & Yankies has Ruined this County so it is
impossible for them to stay here Let me hear from you by the first mail as
what I do I must do promptly Direct your letters to
Valley Town
North Carolina

Yous Best
N.G. Phillips

## G.W. Logan to Dear Sir[6]

Richmond Va
30th May 1864


Dear Sir:

      A few days ago I visited Camp Winder a Hospital near this place & saw some of your countrymen & gained the following information of casualties in the late battle G.S. Ferguson was wounded in the head, not serious M. Main [?] in the elbow L.W. Murray, in the side H.P. Holland in the hand T.M. Green in the arm  The above are the only ones I have heard from.  I am sorry I cannot write you something of interest Congress has done but very little, nor do I think it will do much.  We are trying to modify the Tax T[?] and impressment laws but I cannot as yet tell the result. Genl Lee has fallen back near this place & it is believed his army will soon be within the entrenchments surrounding the City.  It is said Gen Grant is now coming up on the old ground of McClelland & will unite with [?]. Both armys are reinforcing largely [?] & the next fight is expected to be the great battle of the War. In the late engagements the loss on both sides was immense, our loss must have been in Killed wounded & prisoners at least 20 or 25.0000 & the Yankees more than double that number.
      There is but little appearance of Peace, though the present Congress is much stronger for negotiations than the preceding one. The Dis [?] are determined not to have peace only in their own way & at their own time.


Very Respectfully
G.W. Logan

## Col. William Holland Thomas to President Jefferson Davis[7]

Headquarters ,
Strawberry Plains, November 8, 1862.

President Jefferson Davis:

Dear Sir: Summer is gone; fall has come. During the latter we came near losing East Tennessee. At present we have to look out for the future.

I beg leave to submit a plan for the defenses of East Tennessee, which has been submitted to General Jones and others, and received their approval:

1st. Let a depot be established at the west end of the bridge at Strawberry Plains.

2d. Let the road be completed from that point into the road leading to Blain's Cross-Roads.

3d. This would complete the opening of the wagon communication between the East Tennessee and Virginia Railroad and Kentucky.

To Secure this communication to be kept open, I would respectfully recommend the establishment of the line of posts, from 15 to 20 miles apart, on the plan adopted on the road leading from the Mississippi Balley to California. The wagons, by stopping at a post each night, could be protected, which would secure us permanently.

To complete this Communication with Kentucky, a guard of Indians or other soldiers would be necessary to pass from post to post and an old-fashioned block-house should be built at such post to protect our troops against sudden emergencies.

The present prices of salt produce the necessity of putting in operation the goose Creek salt works where coal is in convenient distance to the salt works and fuel. But there is another advantage to be anticipated. It will secure the control of the article of salt in the hands of government agents. That is worth more than 5,000 troops. Besides, it will secure a communication with Southern Kentucky to be kept open, which will facilitate trade in beef, bacon, &c.

Yours, truly,
Wm. H. Thomas
Commanding, Legion of Indians and Highlanders.

107

**Colonel William Holland Thomas**

## Col. William H. Thomas to Gov. Zebulon B. Vance[8]

Knoxville
Nov. 22 1862
[Governor Vance]

 In the progress of the war men and circumstances change. At the commencement you were in the military and I was in Civil positions. Now my position is what your position was then. I find myself at the head of a Regment or Legion of Indians and mountaineers, entrusted with duties in East Tennessee and Kentucky. And as your duties relate principally to the defence of North Carolina permit me to submit for your consideration a few facts believed to be connected with the public services and the defense of the State.

1st Would it not be advisable to make an arrangement to have able bodied negro men belonging to the counties in reach of the enemy employed by the State and transferred from their present positions to work on the extension of the Railroad?

They could, I presume, be employed for the cost on ensurance and food and raiment. By this two objects would be gained. 1st every negro would be saving of $1000, to the owner. 2d Every able bodied negro kept out of the hands of the enemy would lessen the number of troops we have to raise in defence, equal to a saving of at least $1000 per year. Thus if North Carolina employed ten thousand negroes on the road where a small force could keep them in subjection, $10,000,000 would be saved to the owners, and 10,000 men more would defend our cause.

One consideration now animates us all. What will ensure success not what would be most agreeable to us. The Legislature appropriated two millions of dollars to defend Eastern North Carolina and the Western frontiers? Both are now in danger. The western Counties are in danger of being over run by deserters and renegades who by the hundred are taking shelter in the smoky mountains. The men between 35 and 40 west of the Blue Ridge should be furnished with arms and ammunition, and required to aid in guarding their homes. And the Confederate should be required to place Military compys at every trap in the Smoky mountains from Ashe to Cherokee. As long as we can hold the Country encircled by the Blue Ridge and Cumberland mountains and their outside slopes we have the heart of the south, which commands the surrounding Plains. The loss of this country larger than England or France is the loss of the Confederacy and we sink under a despotism.          W. H. Thomas

Haywood County Collections

1. J. Cathey letter to Rev. L.F. Siler, 22 Feb 1861. Joseph Cathey and Cathey Family Papers. Hunter Library Digital Collections, Western Carolina University, Cullowhee, NC.

2. James W. Killian letter to Col. J. Cathey, 19 Jan 1863. Joseph Cathey and Cathey Family Papers. Hunter Library Digital Collections, Western Carolina University, Cullowhee, NC.

3. Emma A. Shoolbred letter to Col Cathey, 30 Mar 1863. Joseph Cathey and Cathey Family Papers. Hunter Library Digital Collections, Western Carolina University, Cullowhee, NC.

4. James B. Rankin letter to Col. J. Cathey, 11 Aug 1863. Joseph Cathey and Cathey Family Papers. Hunter Library Digital Collections, Western Carolina University, Cullowhee, NC.

5. Nathaniel G. Phillips letter to Col. Cathey, 24 Dec 1863. Joseph Cathey and Cathey Family Papers. Hunter Library Digital Collections, Western Carolina University, Cullowhee, NC.

6. G.W. Logan letter to Dear Sir, 30 May 1864. Joseph Cathey and Cathey Family Papers. Hunter Library Digital Collections, Western Carolina University, Cullowhee, NC.

7. Col. William H. Thomas letter to President Jefferson Davis, 8 Nov 1862, Official Records of the Union and Confederate Armies, Ser. I, Vol. 20, pt. II, p. 395.

8. Col. William H. Thomas letter to Gov. Zebulon Baird Vance, 22 Nov 1862, Zebulon Baird Vance (1830-1894) Papers, 1862, NC Digital Collections. State Archives of North Carolina: Civil War Collection.

# 6. HENDERSON COUNTY COLLECTIONS

## Shipman Family Correspondence

Jesse Albert Shipman (1843-1863) was the oldest child of Andrew Robinson Shipman and Sarah Towe of Henderson County, NC. Shipman enlisted on May 20, 1861 with the Buncombe Rangers who were later incorporated into Company G, 1st Regiment NC Cavalry. He was fatally wounded in a cavalry skirmish near Martinsburg, West Virginia in July 1863 and died three days later.

## Daniel W. Revis Letters, 1862-1863, 1865

Daniel Webster Revis (1835-1914) was the son of John Revis and Rebecca Heatherly of Zirconia, NC. He served with Company B, 64th Regiment NC Infantry. After the war, Revis served as a Baptist preacher at Mount Page Baptist Church in 1865 and later Double Springs Baptist Church in 1871. Daniel Revis is buried in the Double Springs community in Henderson County.

Revis's wife was Sarepta Ward, the daughter of Bartlette and Nancy Morgan Ward. Daniel and Sarepta had twelve children. The letters of Sarepta Revis in this collection were written for her by her relatives since she was unable to read or write. Several different examples of handwriting have been identified among her letters confirming that various members of the family were asked to assist her in communicating with her husband.

## Jesse A. Shipman to Andrew R. Shipman[1]

ashevill N C Camp woodfin

June 2 [1861]

Dear father

I take my pen in hand to let you now that I am well at this time hoping that when thes few lines coms to hand that they may find you all well father I am coming home next Saturday I want you to hav me a good horse aganst then if you get me a horse I will get $24 amonth $12 amonth for me doll 12 for my horse go to [?] and try to trad him out of his mare ther are five Companys her now
A Way Down in virgina Wher I dont expect to Dye  load up my gun and make the yankeys fly

I am well satus fied and got plenty to eat I Want apare of pants Dark colerd br tell Avery folks that avery will bat home next Saturday We expect to go to the warm springs in about three weeks we has our pistols her now redy to shot the yankeys that is all that we think about is killing yankes last evning we had a ragement Dress per rad[regiment dress parade] with about 400 hunderd in [?] tell that [?] is well satus fied I must fetch my leter to [?]

A son to A father

## Jesse A. Shipman to Andrew R. Shipman[2]

Camp W. N. Edwards
February the 6.1862

Dear Father

I this morning seat my self to drop you a line in answer to yours of January th 10.1862 it came safe to hand and was rcd with the gratest degree of pleasure in which I was glad to hear that you was all well those lines found mee as well as usual I was varry proud of the presants you sent mee it came in good time things is varry high at manassas socks is worth 50 to 75 cts pur pair and other things in porpotion I hope you will not think hard of mee for not writting to you I was detailed on a 8 days scot and left camp the varry day your letter come I seed a fine time wee just hunted whiskey and pord it out to keep the soldiers from getting it I just got what I could drink and a canteen full to bring in to camp and i can tell you it reigns ever day or snows hear and is the muddiest plase you ever seede and the worst water to use I ever seede allthough wee ar willin to stay till the war ends wee ar like the little Bull at the foddor stack wee ~sy~ say dam them that [?] wee ar not uneasy I think their is the best hope of peace has ever bin ~Col Ramson~ Col. Ransom is looking all the time for an order to give us all furlows the health of our Reg is varry bad wee think their is some hope of them getting better since dr hilliard came home wee lost one man while he was gon to asheville he was a good soldier and A god Boy he was a Boy from Rims Creek buncomb N. C although their is a good eal of sickness yet wee will get our 2 months weges in a day or 2 and their is nearly 9 monts dew us when wee ar in the survis 12 months wee will get 50. dolars bounty and I will send that all home I would asque you to tell all the Boys and esposhely the Gals that I will bee able to come home in a very short time if nothing happons nore than I know of tell Mort. I was varry glad to Get the glovs he sent to mee though they was rather small I think I has got fat since I hav bin in the war Paw pleas have vandavar to make mee a good pare of boots no 8 and send them the 1st one is apassing and I will send you the money when I get it Jackson Stepp sends his best respects and he wants you to tell grandady and gang howdy for mee and all the rest of his friends he says to tell you wee dont fear th d d yankees one bit mee and Stepp has got 7 blankets and one old wagon sheet and wee have fared varry well this witer stepp says ~th~ he has som hops of getting to come home and hee says he will come up Jesse Case [i.e.: Cpl. Jesse Case, Co. G, 1st North Carolina Cavalry] say tell his friends that he is in the land of th living and would like to bee at one more [?] and espeshly a frollic so you will pleas writ soon no more at this time only Remains your obediant son      J.A. Shipman

## Jesse A. Shipman to Andrew R. Shipman[3]

Camp. Wise.
March the 22 1862

my Dear Father .5. sisters

I seat my self to let you that I am well and have reached Richmond one more time wee reached this plase .21.ont and your kind letter came safe to hand in cear of sergt. case. it was red with cear your clothing you sint me Came safe also and unforchantly one bottle of the whiskey you sent got broken I received the other bottle I will tell you there is 2 more man in our co. has died Whos names is Ł John White and L. L. Stepp [i.e.: Pvts. Jonathan B. White and Lewis L. Stepp, Co. G, 1st North Carolina Cavalry] and J. K. P. Shipman Left our co. the 3 day of March and I havent herd from him sence he was varry bad off when he left I think he is in the hospittle at thys plase Dr Hilliord sayd he would try to assertain to day where he was sent and if he is dead I will write to you in hast he was oblige to bee sent to the hospitle for wee cold not take him with us wee have had hard times wee have not stayd one plase more than one night in 4 weeks wee ar now on the road to Goles Burro N. C. our forces at Manassas has fell back Rapihanticick River our reasons for retreating is a varry good one one reason is it was so muddy that wee could not have a fore back with them and another was that wee was cut off they yankees folored our forces to warron va. and their they turned on them and had a right nise little battle our men had the best of the fight they killed Some I cant say how many they took .100. prisners and if the road had not Bin so muddy they would run them to Bulls Run and that is all the War news I have at this time I want you to come to our Reg^t if you think it will bee the best and if their is any other .Co. you had rather go in if you haft to go you need not come to this co. on my account I will tell you if I had to volinteer a gain I would go in a cavlry co. thoug evy mans nothion is not alike I cant thin the war can last vary much longer I hardly think it can hold up so I will clos I will rite to you again when wee get stationed so you need not write till i write a gain yours as ever

J. A. Shipman

Tell Mart I am varry much oblige to him for his glovs [?] sent mee tell him I will get home as soon as can

J. A. Shipman

### A.P. Corn to Andrew R. Shipman[4]

MartinsBurg V.A. July the 20 1863

Mr. A. R. Shipman

I Seat myself this day to drop you a few lins to inform you of the los of
your Son Albert he got Shot am yesterday th 19 in a fight we had [?]
martinsburg V.A. he was Shot in the right Side but whether hit in his in Sids
or not I cant Say for the yankees too him off befor we cold get him out but
if the ball did not not rang in his in Sids I dont think bit dangers W. T.
Boyd was kild in the Sam battal If I hear anything Els about him I will let
you no as Son as I can he went in the battal dismounted to Sharp Shoot and
when he Started in ~~he told~~ told Jackson Kyirkendall [i.e.: Pvt Jacob R.
Kuykendall, Co. G, 1st North Carolina Cavalry]

If he did not get out to tak his Hors and ceap him for him J K P Shipman
was not cone to the Redgment yet but we ar looking for him ever day [?] at
this time but Still Remans yours until Dith

A P Corn to A R Shipman

Pleas [?] this as Soon as you get my letter and let me hear from you

Direct your letters to Winchester Po V.A

## J.K.P. Shipman to Andrew R. Shipman[5]

Culpeper Va
July 25th 1863

Dear Uncle

I take my pen in hand to Let you no that I am well and hop that these fiew Lines may come safe to hand and find you all well I havant aney thing to Right onely hard times Lieut Henery [i.e.: 1st Lt. James L. Henry, Co. G, 1st North Carolina Cavalry] wants to no what you want don with Alberts Horse he is a ~~fine~~ good horse Albert was wonded ~~at~~ and died at martins burg Va I started you a leter this morning I Rote it sevral days ago but could not mail it till this morning Right soon and let us no what you want don with his horse No more at present

Right soon

J. K. P. Shipman

A. R. Shipman

## Daniel Revis to Sarepta Revis[6]

[mid-November 1862]


I take the pesent opotunity to rite you a few lines to let  you no that iam wel at presan  and hoping that thies  few lines wil fnd you  in good helth  I want you to rite to me to let  me no how you and little  slocum is and to let  me no how al your things  is gitting along  you must  do the best you can til I come  home  take good cear of your  self and little slocum  tel John morgan to rite  for you  I hav drawn my boun ty and i wil come and bring it home as soon as ican I hav not time to rite any moreat presant  I re main your af fexinate husband unti [I die]

## Daniel Revis to Sarepta Revis[7]

Daniel Revis to Sarepta Revis

December the 7.1862   Knoxville Tenn

Dier wife

I take my pen in hand to let you no that I am well at presant and hoping thies few lines may find you wel I hav just received your leter in forming mee that our sweet little slocum is dead which giv mee grate troble I was expectin to hear that he was dead when I herd fromhim ever sinc I herd he had the sore thrat I told the boys that he wold never get wel Serrpty dont griev for him for it wont do no good he is gon to rest bles his sweet little soal he is gon to heaven to sweet Jesus whar he wil never suf fer no more hecan not come to us but we can go to him sereptia I want you to prepair to meet me and little slocum in heaven I thought wheni left home I wold see you and little slocum again but I shal never see lit ttle slocum no more hier and I may never se you hier any more but stil I hope I wil but if it was gods wil that I shold not I hope I wil meet you in heaven whair we shal havto part no more I hav praid for you ever since I left home and all our folks and I want you all to pray for mee and I wil not forget you tell father and mother that mitchel has ben left our camps two weeks and I hav not herd fromhim I hav got three leters for him and sent them on to him so now more at pesant only I remain yur affectinate husband until death

DW Reavis to sereptia revis

## Daniel Revis to Sarepta Revis[8]

po
Tenn Anderson .Co. clinton

April the 20 1863


Dier wife

I take the presant opertunitey to drop you a few lines to in form you that I
am as well as common and I do hope that thies few lines may find you well
and doing well  we hav just bin atrip to Jacks burrow and was gon fore days
[Jacksboro in Campbell County, Tennessee] we herd that the yanks was
coming threw the gap and was ordered to march upon afree march in sped
but when we got thair we found no yanks thair but we dont no what our we
may hav to start back to the gap for they say the yanks is close thair and we
dont no when we may hav acumbat with them  the pepel is planting corn
hier and the woods is geting green and it makes me want to be at home
aplanting corn sobad I cant rest but i now I shal get to plant no corn this
yer  sereptia I want you to keep in good hart for I stil hope I wil get to
come home before Agrate while
D W Revis to Sarepta S Revis

show bill the [cower?] sid  soon as you get this


for J [M?] Revis

I hav Just received your kind leter sens I comenst riting this leter  I was glad
to hier that you was wel but I as sorry to hier that georg was ded sereptia
you rote to me to come home  I now I want to come home as bad as you
want me to come but I dont see any chance of geting to come home we hav
Just rceived orders to start back to the gap and I hav to rite in a hurry clint I
am sorry for you and all the rest of your folks for it seemes like they hav
bad luck I want you to ri ite to me as often as you can so i must bring my
rmarks to aclose by saying that I remain your loving husband until deth
D W revis to Sareptia

Dear brother
I rite you afew lines to let you no I am well  I this will find you awl well  I
recevd aletter from poley that you [broat?] [?] an one you sent bill  I want
you to gow thar as soon as you get this an let them  I hav hear from A[?]

but I cant get to come  they wont let nobody off now  we haf to start to Jacks burrow in a few minits  bill go [sertin?]  I will rite as soon as I can get one hours time  I close

J M Revis

## Daniel Revis to Sarepta Revis[9]

The state of cane tuckey wain co [Wayne County, Kentucky]
May th 13 1863


Dier wife

I take the presant time to drop you a few lines to let you no that I am well
at this time we air something over 1 hundred miles from Clinton and air in
about 8 or 10 miles of the yanks and do expect every day when we wil come
in contact with them we air in 8 miles of the cumberlan river thair is three
ridgments of us together and we air under col farmer acting as generl we
air in a bewiful part of the world sereptia I am a long ways from home but
I am not out of hart yet I hope I will get to come home again I want you
to take good car of your self we have had a hard march to get heer and has
had more rivers to waid thani ever saw we hav bin twelv days on the rode
friends I want you to rite to me and let me no hw you air geting along
direct your leters to clinton and they wil follow the redgment we cotch
atory as we came on and kild him and the tories shot at our boys and shot
one threw the hat bwt did not hirt hime sereptia i dowant to see youvery
bad and and all therest of the folks but I dont no whether I will ever hav
the plesur of meting with you any more on erth or not but if I dont I want
you to prepair to mete mee in heaven so I must bring my leter to aclose by
saying that I remain your loving husban til deth

D W Revis to Sareptia S revis

### Sarepta Revis to D.W.Revis[10]

NC Henderson County June the 7 1863

My Dear loveing Husband

I am bless with the presant time to drop you afew lines to inform you that I am well at this time and I do hope and trust that theas few lines may finde you enjoying the same like blessing  I receive your letter yes terday with plesure I was so glad to hear from you but I am sorry to hear that you have got so faroff from me  I have bad news to rite to you at this time for the war has commence hear at last  thear was 15 of Capt Casees men come home  three Statons  three Longs  bob Beding field and sevral others and out of 15 about [chalk?] has gone back  Liutenant garron come after them and got about half of them to goe back  the statons aint gone back nor tha never will all go back Liutenant garron tuck sevral men with him and went after ruben and Ambers Staton and one of them shot garron and kill him he dident live more than hour and half  then the men that was with garron shot at rube and Ambers and wounded them but tha never got them but Ambers wound kill him  he only live about one day and night and rube was wouned in the shoulders and I dont no whear he is  I hear that the men is runing a way fast hear of late and the malishey [militia] is out a trying to gether them up but tha come slowe speed at it for tha aint gott but four or five yet and tha hav been gone aweek and tha say that the runaways sends word to Col [?]ned that tha wil meet him in any old field and take afight with him and his men but tha aint done it yet nor I dont beleive tha will for I thinck tha  are [boull?] afraid to come in contack with each other  thare is more dezerters than thare is malishey hear but some of them has gone angive up to go back I am sory to hear that was in Kentucky I am afraid I never will get to see you any more on earth for I hear that the yanckeys has run you all back agood ways  I aint rote to you in two weeks for I hear that you had left clinton I have move to fathers and clint and Ellen has move there too  I want you to rite to me soon and offen as you can  so no more but far you Well for this time

Sarepta S Revis
to D. W. Revis

## Henderson County Collections

1. Jesse A. Shipman letter to Andrew R. Shipman, 2 Jun 1861. Rare Books and Special Collections: Manuscripts of the American Civil War, Hesburgh Library, University of Notre Dame, Indiana.

2. Jesse A. Shipman letter to Andrew R. Shipman, 6 Feb 1862. Rare Books and Special Collections: Manuscripts of the American Civil War, Hesburgh Library, University of Notre Dame, Indiana.

3. Jesse A. Shipman letter to Andrew R. Shipman, 22 Mar 1862. Rare Books and Special Collections: Manuscripts of the American Civil War, Hesburgh Library, University of Notre Dame, Indiana.

4. A.P. Corn to Andrew R. Shipman, 20 Jul 1863. Rare Books and Special Collections: Manuscripts of the American Civil War, Hesburgh Library, University of Notre Dame, Indiana.

5. J.K.P. Shipman to Andrew R. Shipman, 25 Jul 1863. Rare Books and Special Collections: Manuscripts of the American Civil War, Hesburgh Library, University of Notre Dame, Indiana.

6. Daniel Revis to Sarepta Revis, Nov 1862. NC Digital Collections. State Archives of North Carolina: Civil War Collection.

7. Daniel Revis to Sarepta Revis, 7 Dec 1862. NC Digital Collections. State Archives of North Carolina: Civil War Collection.

8. Daniel Revis to Sarepta Revis, 20 Apr 1863. NC Digital Collections. State Archives of North Carolina: Civil War Collection.

9. Daniel Revis to Sarepta Revis, 13 May 1863. NC Digital Collections. State Archives of North Carolina: Civil War Collection.

10. Sarepta Revis to D.W. Revis, 7 Jun 1863. NC Digital Collections. State Archives of North Carolina: Civil War Collection.

# 7. JACKSON COUNTY COLLECTIONS

## Major Wiley Parris Civil War Letters

Major Wiley Parris of Jackson County, North Carolina, was 37 when he enlisted in May, 1861 in Jackson County. He served as a private in the North Carolina 25th Infantry Regiment, Company B. The letters in this collection are all addressed to his wife, Jane Parris. According to *North Carolina Troops, vol. 7, p. 376*, Wiley was discharged shortly after his letter of July 3, 1862, "by reason of being over age," but according to the Civil War Index of the 25th NC Infantry, Parris was killed on July 1, 1862 at Malvern Hill. The Federal Census of 1860 for Jackson County, North Carolina, lists an M.W. Parris, age 36, and Jane Parris, age 34, as his wife. Note that Parris's first name, Major, is his given name and not a military rank.

## James Watson Collection

The collection contains two letters to James Watson, a Confederate soldier in the 25th NC Regiment, from his wife, Elizabeth Watson, and a friend, Alfred Wilson. The Watsons and Wilson were residents of Hamburg, Jackson County, North Carolina. In the first letter, dated October 29, 1861, Elizabeth Watson writes of missing her husband, food prices, crop conditions, the scarcity of money, the family, deaths in the county, and the weather. The second letter, written by Alfred Wilson, was dated March 8, 1862. Wilson comments on food prices, the invasion of the South by Northern troops, and his desire for victory and peace.

## Major Wiley Parris to Janie Parris[1]

febuary the 6 1862

Camp Lee
grahamville South Carolina

dear wife

it is with pleasur that I avail my Self of the presant opportunity of writing
you a few lines to let you know that I am well at this time hoping thes lines
will find you in the best of health I received a leter las monday Evening
which gave mee great sattis faction to hear from you that you Still had bin
well you Stated that you had hird a  boy to Stay with you tel I Come home
and you wanted to now som thing about making a Crop you Can put him
to Sprouting and Cleaning up grond tel time to plow  Sow down the all the
ould [?] pece in oats and get redy for plowing as son as the weather will do I
Started a leter last monday morning and I want to now what days my leters
gits thar I have bin writing every Sunday and the leter leaves her on monday
now tel mee what day you git them and I will now when to rite

I Can in form you that we have had now fite yet but the yankes Came out
nite befor last and kild one of the pickets and Cripeld another but not our
men the was horsemen that was about tel miles from her and one of the
pickets kild three yankes and the yankes went back in the Iland I Cant tel
you when we wil git off I think we fill [?] git off a ginst fifteen of April I
Can in form you that we have not drawd any mor money yet and I don't
now when we will you will haft to hire som man to Chop up your bigest
logs and to plow the first day for I am a frad that the boy will let my horse
runaway I want you to pay Cope that note and less the note it was eight
dollas some sents and what I owe him on the books you Can let that a lone
tel I com home and I want you to git that note I give T T S Sherrel

the health of our men is god at this time we have one in the hospitel and we
are looking for him in Camp tl tel Mr grimes that justus is well and harty I
want you to write how your Corn holds out I have nothing Strang to write
at this time mor then I want to See you very bad and the time seams long to
mee but in two months mor I think I will be on the road home and if I haft
to Stay my time out it will Soon run off now I have not bin weat Sence I
left Ashville I have bin on picket on time and one time mor will do mee tel
my time is out I don't see any prospect of a fite though we Can hear the
Cannas evry weake and some times mor all of the Connection well So

nothing mor at this time onley I remain your affectionat husband un tel
death

Wiley Parris to Jane Parris

## Major Wiley Parris to Jane Parris[2]

State of NC   Lenoir County

kinston
April the 13 1862

dear wife

it is with pleasur that I take the presant opportunity of writing you a few
lines to let you now that I am well at this time hoping thes lines will find
you in good health I hant any thing strang to rite at this time more then I
want to sse you verry bad we hant had any fite yet and I don't think we will
have we are stationed 5 miles from kinston and has got Chimneys to our
tents and is doing tolerabel well though it does look like that old ransom
will drill us to death all the Connection is well only [?, crease in page ] he
has had a pain in his head but is giting beter mee and Alfred boath has bin
Sick but has got well a gin the last leter I got was when the Campt Com I
am lookng for a leter every day though I now that you Cant take time to rite
often nor I don't want you to try to rite verry often for I Cant rite much my
Self for I am out of paper and in vellops and Stamps I only have a nuf to
rite one more leter I got a leter from  m montieth and Cant anser him for
want of paper thar is Chance for us to git off tel our time is out I don't
think but forty seven days will soon run  Run off and then our time will be
out when you rite tel mee how you are giting a long with your work and
how your stock looks and I want you to have mee a good mess of eggs
aginst I Com home for I have lived on bread and meet tel I am tired of hit
and I want a good Jug of whiskey with som Cherry tree bark in hit for I
now I will need som  thar has bin a talk of keeping us in longer than our
time but I don't think that will be don  tha made us send all of our things to
golds boro that we Could do with out for we all thoght that we would have
a fite when we first Com her and we may have yet be for we leve her the
yankes in thirty miles of us it is not worth my while to try to tel you how
bad I want to See you for I Could not if I was to rite all day So I will Close
for the presant I Still remain your affectonate
husband tel death


M W Parris to Jane Parris

## Major Wiley Parris to Jane Parris[3]

July the 3 1862  peters burg, va
dear wife

I one time mor take my pen in hand to let you now that I am well at this
time hoping thes lines may find you well and doing well the last leter I
received was dated June the 7 it give mee great Sattis faction to hear from
you that you was well though I am sorry to tel that Som of our brave boys
has got kild and Severl wounded in the great battle at richmond which
Commenct last wensday and is Still fiting yet we have not got a correct
information of all the file neither Can I tel all ded and wonded but I will
[strikethrough] tel what I have larnd a bout it giled long and John B. queen
was Seen fall in the first of the fite that is all that we now of though thar
was a great many missing [Eith ?] kild of or lost now I will give the names
of what was wonded Joseph moody got to fingers shot off William Cogdal
wonded in the neck leander hall in the lage harris hooper in the thy or lage
[strikethrough] Samuel Parker Slitly wonded in the finger though hot his
Sholder out of place and from what he Ses a bout the redgment it is but all
up parker left them yesterday morning and ses that the redgment looks a
bout as big as as four or five Companys our Cournel got five or six holes
Shot threw his Cote and one Cut his face major frances badly wonded in
the Sholder  w william beard badly wonded threw the hips Capt Coalman
his head shot off with a ball that is all I have heard of the 16 redgment our
men has whipt them evry fite and has drove them Severl miles and has
taken a Site of prisners with som six Jennerls and has kild Scors of them I
under Stand that all of our men is bured but the is laying in piles and not
bered a tall I think that we will the victry but dearly bought Severl of our
men got ther gun Shot in too in thier hands  the  the boys has lost ther
blankets in the fite tha have bin gon a about eight days frm Camp I Cant tel
when tha will Com back and one of our men did in the hospitel da befor
yesterday david wilson and severl is in the hospitel yet A W parris is with
the rest in the fite I hant heard any thing a bout him parker did not now
hoo all was mising this is all I Can find out a bout the fite I was left to gard
Camp James is not well he has bin punity Severl weaks I hant any thing
Elce to write at this time mor then I want to See you verry bad but I Cant
tel when I will be blest with that blesing it wont be long tel my time will be
out a gin but I Cant tel whether I will  gt  git to Com or not I hant heard
any thing sed a bout that times is two hot her now I am a frade for mee to
git off I will rite a gin in a few days so nothing mor may the lord bles you
and thake Care of you is my prays and has bin ever sence I left you

M W Parris to Jane Parris

## Elizabeth Watson to James Watson[4]

Oct 29 1861
North carolina Jackson Co

Dear friend and husband

it is with grate pleasure that i rite to you to let you now that mea and my
children is well hoping these few lins will find you in good health  I have
Just red the leter that you sent mea and was glad to her that you was alive
But you did not say whether you was well or not  But I hope you was  I
have red 4 leters from you and has rot you 2 and my dear I hant forgot you
for i think of you every hour in the day and would all most give up my life if
you could bea back at home to stay with mea and your children for Alexand
talks about you a many atime   times in our county is hard for the poor class
of people for every thing is giting so deer that tha cant By hardly a naughf
to [enough to] gan [?] an salt is from nine to ten dollars a sack her and every
other thing is proportion thier is good crops made in our county  I think
corn can bea bought at 50 cts all through the winter and now this people is
debard [?] of halling off thir meet  I dont now how wee will git our
nessaryes for money is scerce here  I have got all of our property yet  I have
not sold eny of it yet and I think that I will keep it for i cant sell it for its
worth only Bacon or Beef catle and I hant got eny of that so turn over your
fathers folks is all well and giting along very well  allison is a working for
mea and epects to work 10 or 12 (?) days  he has left home and expects to
marry before he gos back  he is a talking of coming to you but I think it is
all a Joke [?] is making a good crop of corn and is milking 2 cows thar are
increesing and doing well franklin was up a bout a week a go and tha was all
well and franklin has a fine son miss Mckiney is deed has Bin dead some 4
weeks   thir has bin several deths in our county and her dying words was
pray for mea  S I Calhoun came clare of killing crane thir is 3 company of
volenteers made up in macon county one starts to day thir capt is Alfred
Bell and allen amons will start before long wea have quite wram wither
[warm weather] her for this time of year and the most rain i ere saw of afall
wee have had some frost  But it hanet done now inJury  thir is good crops
made in hamburg but it is to warm and wet to gether yet  I hope ther will
Bea a chang of Wether for a litle cooler Wither would Bea the Best and
perhaps would bea helther for you my deer I wish I could see you Wee
could have a heep of good fun  look on nex page hold on till I git a nother
lamp for my lite is Bad har I have got more talow and now i will rite on  I
would like to have your likness  But the people ses that I have got it with
mea for thae saz that Elizabeth hamton is a young gim  James Franklins
helth is a Bout like it was When you left  John T[?] folks is all well an ant

fany sed to send you howdy for her  F.A. Hoopers Funeral was preecht last sabath By Corn From Henderson so I must come to a close By saying that I hope I will see you When your time is out so fare well

To James Watson
Elizabth Watson
T.A.(?) Watson
J.F.(?) Watson
E. Hamton Watson

There is howdy for mea and all of your children her is your shoo strings if you a git them

### Alfred Wilson to James Watson[5]

Hamburg N.C. Jackson County
March the 8th 1862

Mr. James Watson

Dear Friend

I now seat my self this plesant eavening to inform you that wee are all well at presant   hoping these lines will come to hand and find you and friends all well  I recieved yourse of feb the 17th and was glad to hear that you and friends was all well Dear sir I would like to see you a gain but the time doo not permit you have nobly responded to our countrys call of which perhaps I would bee with you if times would permit or at least if my health was good.  the foe is invadeing our soil and you are nobly standting in her defence and if the opertunity offers I think you all will serve the foe just right that is to make them wheel about and take the step that is called doubel quick or else by your exerciouns they tumble down like they ought to bee served I must rite something a bout times here they acks seventy five cts for corn here bacon 12½ cts a pound  salt 20 dollars a sack.  they are a making up a nother company in Jackson  doctor sensaboy is the capt  thare has several voanteard in the company  I understand george shook has volanteard  monroe hooper  dave woodring  john parker  dave mathis  I understand they loud to finish making up their company to day at webster they wanted one hundred and thirty men in Jackson County and two hundred and forty men in macon County it looks like taking nearly all the men out of the country but wee must stand to the storm of war to defend our country from the stubern foe to keep them back from our soil and finaly I hope to preserve liberty and peace forever and you can return in peace to your homes a gain to your welcome ing fathers and mothers wives and brothers and sisters who will rejoice to see you come back a gain to live and cultivate your native land.  please write when you recieve these lines give us the nues in jineral and a bout your fare and a bout the growth of the country.  pleese reed this note adr address to all the friends I call you friends because you all stand in my defence as well as your own and I love and thank you all forit  like wise all the good soldiers in the sothern confederacy so I must come to a close by subscribe ing my self and your friend til death

Alfred Wilson written to James Watson and Friends

Jackson County Collections

1. Major W. Parris letter to Jane Parris, 6 Feb 1862. Major Wiley Parris Civil War Letters. Hunter Library Digital Collections, Western Carolina University, Cullowhee, NC.

2. Major W. Parris letter to Jane Parris, 13 Apr 1862. Major Wiley Parris Civil War Letters. Hunter Library Digital Collections, Western Carolina University, Cullowhee, NC.

3. Major W. Parris letter to Jane Parris, 3 July 1862. Major Wiley Parris Civil War Letters. Hunter Library Digital Collections, Western Carolina University, Cullowhee, NC.

4. Elizabeth Watson letter to James Watson, 29 Oct 1861. James Watson Collection. Hunter Library Digital Collections, Western Carolina University, Cullowhee, NC.

5. Alfred Wilson letter to James Watson, 8 Mar 1862. James Watson Collection. Hunter Library Digital Collections, Western Carolina University, Cullowhee, NC.

# 8. MACON COUNTY COLLECTIONS

## Edmonston and Kelly Families Collection

In this collection, the "Maggie" who writes the letter is Magdaline Bryson and the deceased husband she mourns was Rufus Alexander Edmonston (1828-1863). The Edmonstons were married on November 4, 1853. According to the letter, they have lost a child, and research bears this out. There is a headstone in the Cullowhee Baptist Church cemetery marked "Dr. R.A. Edmonston" and next to it is a small stone of similar age with the name "Little Charley."

Maggie Edmonston speaks of a "Capt. Grady" in her letter. One William S. Grady, 25th NC Regiment, who previously served as Captain of Company G was appointed Major on December 18, 1862, and transferred to the Field and Staff. According to reports, he was present or accounted for until wounded in the right arm, left arm and right breast at the Crater, near Petersburg, Virginia, July 30, 1864. Grady was hospitalized at Petersburg until October 14, 1864, when he was furloughed. He died in Greenville, South Carolina, October 20, 1864, from a fever and wounds.

## C. W. Slagle Collection

The Siler family resided in Macon County and were wealthy land and slave owners. In 1860, Julius Siler built his home, known as Dixie Hall, on Franklin's main street. Siler was one of the men who served in the Confederate Army, probably enlisting in Macon County in 1861 and being commissioned as a captain. Julius was wounded in battle, but returned home at the close of the war. He died on June 8, 1866.

Siler's mansion, Dixie Hall, holds a special place in Confederate history. The final surrender of the Confederate Army in North Carolina is believed to have taken place at Dixie Hall on May 12, 1865. It was there that Col Stephen Whitaker surrendered the last of the Thomas Legion to Col. George W. Kirk of the 3rd NC Mounted Infantry. Dixie Hall was torn down in the 1970s to make room for the Macon County Courthouse.

D.H. Gettys was closely connected with the Siler family. He served in the 9th Regiment North Carolina Troops (1st Regiment NC Cavalry), enlisting in May 1861 at Macon and dying in March 1862. In the Gettys letters on display at Western Carolina University in Cullowhee, NC, he describes the terrible events which he and his fellow soldiers witness regularly. He also writes of remembering his home in Franklin and wishing to make it back though the war so he can return to it.

## Maggie Edmonston to Dear Brothers B.B. & B.F.[1]

Webster NC July 14th 1864

Dear Brothers B.B. & B.F.

It has been a long time since I have written to you. I have written you several times but it seems like my letters never reaches you from some cause I am not able to tell the cause on however you never acknowledge the reception of a single letter from me but not withstanding that I will write you again to let you know I have not forgotten you. There is not a day passes but you occupy a place in my memory. I very often think of passed pleasures when we used to enjoy each others society together with those loved ones who are gone. Dear brothers it has been a long time since I saw either of you. There has been so many changes taken place so many loved ones have passed away to be no more. when I commence writing I am so perfectly lost in thought, I can scarcely compose my mind to write anything. but what the Lord has done we can not undo. if we could how quick we would do it. I have often wished I could see you and talk with you if I could compose myself but some times when I meet up with my friends it brings recollections of the past so fresh to my mind I am compelled to give vent to my feelings. Oh brothers you can't imagine the heart rending troubles I have had since I last saw you & they are as great to night as they were the day [night] your dear brother left this world to be no more of course I can control my feelings better than I did then but Oh how my poor weary heart sinks when I think that dear one of my bosom is gone forever, one that I looked to for support and protection. how can I realize it. you have lost a good brother, a kind and affectionate brother who took so much interest in your welfare both spiritual & temporal. You all miss him but I must say you can't miss him like I do oh I think of the hopes of by gone days and of the faces I used to love and of the dear one who took so much interest in my welfare, one who was ever ready to comfort me when in distress. I often think of those happy moments and of the joys that have passed away while a shadow deep as the gloom of night falls on my heart's cold hearth. if it was not for the hope I have of one day meeting my beloved friends where there is no more wars or heart rending my poor heart would sink with in me. I some times try to fain [feign] enjoyment and then my heart sickening troubles will come upon me. I don't feel like I ever [even?] would enjoy life any more. Earth has no chances for me but I have stronger ties in Heaven than earth [ever?]. I am often made to wonder if we will ever meet on Earth any more, or if our next meeting will be at the [?] [han?] of God if so I trust we may all be shining Angels. prepare to meet your brother in that happy land for I think If there is a saint in Heaven he is one. he did [died] in the full triumphs of a living faith in Christ. Oh what great comfort to his mourning friends. I have lost a loving brother but the loss of my brother was nothing to compare with the loss of an ffectionate companion. I will beg to change my subject for fear I will make you feel more melancholy than is necessary if I could save you and could compose my self I could talk a great deal to you. I wish this cruel war would close so we could all enjoy each others society once more. I dont get to here from you often. I rc.d a letter from Father & Mother and one from brother Thom also the other day you can't imagine the great amount of pleasure it afforded me to hear from them all and also to hear from you they stated in their letters they had heard from you on Apr 19th[?] and you were both well and had been preserved thru another battle I was very uneasy about you. I hope you may be protected and preserved thru this war and be permitted to enjoy the comforts of home and the society of your friends again. I have nothing of much interest to write you times have been very hard here this summer. crops looks fine. wheat crops are tolerably good. No late war news. have no reliable news from Johnston's Army in Ga [Georgia] we have heard he has given the Yanks a good thrashing on the 27th cut them up badly taken 30 or 40,000 prisoners don't know how come [true?] I have two brothers there in the 39th NC Regt I am very uneasy about them. Sam is a prisoner at Camp Douglas. brother Tom was exchanged and sent home and his health has improved some. He has gone back to headquarters at the forks of Pigeon Haywood NC. brother[?] has gone back to sins [service?]. I fear he will not stand it long. Newt is down at Walhalla SC Father Mother & myself are very lonely if you get home any more you must come and see us. I think I will go out to Haywood in a month or two. I haven't been there in six months. I expect to visit Father & Mother Edmonston whenever I can make it convenient. as long I live and they do I feel it my duty to do so I would not be forgotten by any of you I could write a great deal more but I fear I will weary you reading this uninteresting letter write soon give me all the news write me how Capt Gradys Co is doing if he has a good co or not may Heaven's choicest blessings rest on you both in the prayer of your almost broken hearted Sister

Maggie Edmonston

NB brothers B B an BF
will you please go to the marble yard in Petersburg or any yard you may see and select some nice Tombstones for Dr. Edmonston's grave. I have sent off three times but failed to get any. I know you will take more interest

than any buddy else please let me know if you get any so I can send you the inscription if you can get some nice ones let me know I can have them shipped to Walhalla.  I want two set one Small set for my baby that is all I can do for him and I never will be satisfied until I get that done

Maggie E.

[Note at top of letter]:
BBE
NB [?] sends his regards to you said tell you to hang and kill all the Yankees and come home and go with him to dig gold
M E

## D.H. Gettys to Mrs. A.H. Slagle[2]

Centreville Va
Dec 24th 1861


Mrs A. H. Slagle

In obedience to your request I will try to write you a few lines as to our trip comeing here   we were a long time on the road but we all got here safe and we found the Boys all well but G. [T.?] [Wyont?] he is quite sick but I think not dangerous the boys were as proud to get their things from home as [I was?] [?] any body these was a general shows for joy all through the camps their coats never could have come in a beter time they got here on Saturday evening and the company had to go on picket Sunday   I went with them myself we had a rough time that knight it rained all knight and next morning a heavy sleet fell As you wanted to know about picketing I will tell you all I can   We haev to stay out one day and knight   there are 7 [?] men to each post   there are two men sent out as bidits [?] they have to stand 2 hours at a time then they are relieved by 2 others   they are relieved every two hours during the 24   they are now permited to have fire at the back posts where the [bidits; volis?] can fall back to every 2 hours and warm 4 hours

As to camp life I have not found it any harder than I expected   I am massing [?] the Cartoogechaye boys now   I have not got in to any regular mess yet we expect to move to morrow 6 or 8 miles back from here and go in to winter quarters. Dec 25th our move to day is paid off I don't know now [?] we will move We went out on [?] for the first time since I have been here I liked the fun very well. If you come be [?] the boys [?] breakfass on a fine you would [?] off one [?] I have never said any thing to head it [?] any life they have one big laugh after another from the time they begain it [?] until they are done   it is gatch and [?] all the time myself and Sidney Slagle has just [?] from taking [?] to the Hospital I think he will [?] much better in hospital than in camp he is in every good house one mile from this [?] I think he will get better attention than we could give him here.  The [?] & Thomas are all well they look as well as ever you them and all in fine spirits. I have about a pretty good [?] Bridle & Saddle I have got the Cold Saddle it is a little extra

The day that I came in to camp there was a battle about 12 miles from here our men went out [?] a [?] expedition and were not prepared to fight the Yankees met them [?] overwhelming force drove the [?] back our men being compowered [?] to retreat it is said we [?] 39 men killed and a good many wounded The citizens living near the Battleground think The Yankees had more men killed than we had Although they had all advantaged they made but One day is not obsess [?] more than another  these is no preaching hear I am sorry to say it is to some [?] say they have not heard [?] In 3 months it is hard for a man to live Here and [?] his morals like at home While [?] far away from home one deprived of the priviledeges I once enjoyed I hope you will all remember me in your prayers at all times.  James Siler sends his love to you and family.  I would like to hear how Roxie's foot has got.  Give my love to all my friends I am now in good health and [spirits ?] I would like to hear from home soon

With respect I am yours
D.H. Gettys

To Mr. A.H. Slagle.

Dec 27th We moved yesterday the col says he will go in to winter quarters near where we are now camped

## D.H. Gettys to His Brother[3]


Dec 27th 1861
Dear Brother

I recd your letter and present by Gettys. You could not have sent me any
thing of the same value that would be worth more to me than the boots
my feet were scarcely ever dry before I got them Although I had never
written any thing on the subject yet I thought you would send them and so
expressed to some of the boys nearly a month before they came. I could
not bye such a pair here for less than twenty five or thirty Dollars. Hides
are plenty here but there are no tanneries or at least I have not heard of any.
I can not express my
gratitude and will leave it for you to imagine. We are in a very muddy
country and good boots cant be got by the soldiers. We expect to go to
work in a few days building cabbins for winter quarters. I don't know
exactly how large we will build them but if we make these large enough for
seven we will take Gettys into our mess. There has been some wrong
impressions at home about our little fight, first the No of Yankees killed
was greatly exaggerated. One hundred less than the No published would
cover all that I saw, and as Zeb Vance says 'I was thar" Though I have no
doubt but we killed a good many whom we did not find. I heard
of two being found in the cedars a few days afterwards. In the second place
that tale about my horse being
killed or falling and hurting me was all a lie. I was riding the Wm Angel
Roane and he ran through in fine style. No doubt but you have heard this
of the battle at Dranesville. I went out there next day. We expected to get
another fight but were disappointed The Cowards were satisfied with a
meagre victory over one tenth of their no and after rifling the pockets of
the [killed?] tired [retired?]

I never saw and hope I never again may see such a sight as I saw there.
Our noble Southerners who dared stand up for their rights against an over
whelming odds were lying in heaps covered with their own and fellow's
frozen gore. One poor fellows head was taken off just at the end of the
nose by a cannonball, Another just at the shoulder several others shot in the
head with musket balls &c &c. To be in a battle is of course exciting &
victory stimulates but I never wanted to fight half as bad as I did that day. I
never wanted to see a buck [?] where I was at a stand [?] so bad as I there
wanted to see the yankees. My blood boils to revenge those poor fellows
who were so ated [?] the day before. I think if I ever get another change at
the hireling [?] cowards what I saw there will give double strength to my

arms. Tomorrow we go on picket and stay two nights. Thereafter we will stay out nights at a time. [?]ed stay in eight which I think [?]beter than only staying out only [?] in [?]

Now that I have got my boots over coat and flannels I don't mind picketing like I used to. Tell Pa Sister and Rufus that I will write them all as soon as I can. In the mean time give them my love. I hope that Lou is in Macon by this time, and if so any kindness shown her will be highly appreciated by me. Henderson wants to write a little and I will give way. Please write soon to Your Affectionate Brother

T.S. Siler

P.S. Direct your letters to Manassas care of Capt Siler 1st Reg NC Car. T.S.S.

Mr D W
Dear Sir after 20 long days on the road I got in to camp I went out on picket one day we had a fine day of rain and Sleet tomorrow we have to go out again to stay two days I am getting along pretty well Better than I expected We are coughing big coughs to Night I cant write to Night please excuse these Remarks I will write you when I can

Yours
D H Gettys

## D.H. Gettys to D.W. Siler[4]

Manassas Virginia
Jan 5th 1862

Mr D W Siler

Dear Sir

As this is the first opportunity I have had in the past week to send or write after reading a lesson I have concluded to write you to pass off the time We have been very busy building our cabbins the past week We have got the walls all up ready for covering: if we did not have to go on picket this week we would get them nearly completed   Tuesday we have to go out and stay three days.  I doubt very much whether we stay in our quarters after they are built long enough to pay us for half the trouble we have been at building.  Our company are mostly resting but Some of the companies are working on their houses to day the same as they would any other day. While I was at home I tried to imagine the condition of those in the army but I could not come any where near it although I have not found the duties I have to perform any harder than I expected I have been on guard but one time I have escaped guard by being detailed to work on the houses

Our fare is not such as you have at home   We have wheat bread crackers and beef and it not very well prepared I seldom ever see any corn bread.  If I could have a hoecake baked at home now for dinner it would be a great dessert. I don't know whether I shall see any such thing as pork in camps or not  Some say we will get nothing but beef this winter our beef is generally tolerable good.  When we get our houses built we will have eight men to each mess I have got in with the the Cartoogechaye boys  Our mess is composed of T.S.  W.T. & J.W. Siler  McGillespie W.D. Crawford Soggy & Bud [?] Shields & Myself What is to become of the people and country I don't know it is nothing uncommon to hear of two or three deaths the same day   horses are lying about dead every direction you go.  I have no idea that the state of affairs are half as bad now as they will be by the first of April If this war continues long I think we will have to move to some other portion of the coun try for we will eat up burn up and destroy every thing that is here  the scenes that are here are indescribable.  The exposure we have to undergo is great  not withstanding all that I have not regreted in the least that I joined the service  I may never live to get too old Macon again but if I ever do I know I shall feel better than I would if I had stayed at home Although I have many trials and temptations to undergo I hope to be able to overcome them all I have less changes here for reading

than I ever had any where  Sometimes I have as I think a few minutes time
to read perhaps by the time I get my book there will be a call for something
else which has always to be obeyed.  I hope this unholy war will end soon
but I fear it will cost the lives of thousands first While I am writing here my
mind is running back to the time when last I saw you in Franklin of all the
parting I had to do there was none so hard as to part with you and John
Siler  that was the only time  but what I could controle myself your Uncle
John said something to me I know not what I could neither hear nor speak
I often think of the quiet hours I have spent in Macon.  I hope to live to get
back there to enjoy myself again as in past days Alex Ledford has had
measles but he is getting better  John Wyont has fever but the doctor says
he is getting better  Thomas Theodo. & James are all unwell but able to go
about it is cold mostly that ails them  I have bad cold myself I am well
pleased with my Capt as I could be  Remember me to all my friends
especially to you Pa & Sister

Yours Truly
D.H. Gettys

P.S.
I have sent my likeness to you by Mr Leach if any of my friends wants to
see it you can show it to them and when you have a chance you will please
send it to Mother

D.H. Gettys

**Dixie Hall built by Julius Siler. Macon County, NC.**

## D.W. Siler to Capt. Bell[5]

Franklin Jan 23d 1862

Capt Bell

Dr Sir

Allow me as a friend to address you a few lines in regard to a matter that has caused some excitement in Macon. And first I will say that those who know me best know that from the first I have been a friend to your company. I knew that you experience in Mexico would enable you to command a company better than I could. And I thought that you were entitled to the honor. I still think so. And I am willing to do any thing for your company that its honor requires. Some of your men went to Mr McDowells the other day fired at Thomas [?] with pistols cursing him for a Lincolnite in the presence of his sisters and brought him to town a prisoner with the intention of putting him in jail. You know how easy a matter it is to make even quiet men fight when women are imposed upon. No sensible man will object to the law being carried out in a soldier like manner. And if Tom McDowell is bound by law to go into the service although he is probably not able to stand camp service he must go if you require it that is certain There is no disposition here to rebel against law. The report was going yesterday that a certain man had a company ready to rescue the prisoners I know that man well and heard him say all the time that he would fight for the law whenever that could be found out. And he advised every body to not interfere with volunteers when doing a lawful act but would die before women should be insulted by volunteers or any body else. But the talk about armed resistance is all stuff. No one has thought of such thing

Taking Tom McDowells health into consideration I believe it would be honorable to let him off if it can be done according to law. If not he will go into the regular service. He thinks that your company could not treat him as a fellow soldier after dragging him there by force. Bill McConnel and Jasper Dills allege that they never authorized their names to be enrolled. If such is the fact it would endanger the parties who would arrest them. For the civil law is still in force But you know the facts and will no doubt do what is right

Yours Truly
D.W. Siler

You can show this to any one of your company if you choose

## David W. Siler to Mattie[6]

Franklin Macon Co N.C.
March 21st 1862

Dear Miss Mat

I shall not trouble you with a letter, but a mere note of enquiry. By
extending a trip that I expect to take soon
I can probably, with very little inconvenience, be at your fathers about the
19th or 20th of next month. Will you be at home? If so, and I am not
becoming a troublesome acquaintance, you may expect to see me. That I
may receive your answer before leaving this place please make it as early as
convenient.

Truely Yours
D.W. Siler

### David W. Siler to Mattie[7]

Near Franklin May 5th / 62

My Dear Mat

There was nothing said about writing when we parted but I am glad to know that the time of uncertainty has gone by and that I may now address you without doubt or hesitation. I view the circumstances that led to our acquaintance as being exceedingly fortunate for me. You can form no just idea as to the change that has come over me. It might seem strange to you were I to attempt to describe that change [?] to the time when I returned to your Fathers from West Tennessee I had for some time been trying to school my heart to what seemed to be its fate a life uncared for. It is not my habit to be making appeals for sympathy. I always deemed it more manly to conceal a feeling of sadness and drive it away. But there can be nothing wrong in my confessin to you now that for a while before we first met there seemed very little for me to live for. True little Roxie was here but the thought of her brought with it the recollection of many things for her to learn that I have no art to teach. Mine are the best of friends but all being occupied by matters of their own I often seemed friendless in the very midst of friends. I did not feel so on that night of my return from the west. When I had spoken of the effects of a little exposure in West Tennessee you did an act of kindness that you may have thought nothing of since. I shall never forget it. I had suspected it before but then I knew that you had full possession of my heart

I saw Mr B and made an arrangement without having to spake to any one else. I think now that I shall go by way of Cleaveland taking the cars there. The road on the other rout being exceedingly bad. In every little arrangement it will be my pleasure to conform as nearly as possible to your wishes. And all pains will be taken to supply as far as I can the great loss you sustain in parting with friends. It is my wish that your friends should seem as near to you as they have ever been. While it will be my greatest happyness should I be found worthy the place of your nearest friend. – You were very much mistaken if you thought I was provoked when you made a suggestion the other evening about a little matter of arrangement. No no. If I were to ever differ with you in opinion about any thing and after thinking the matter over should still differ I should tell you so frankly. But when you made that suggestion I began to think and very soon came to the conclusion that you were right. Indeed what I said at first was more to get your views than from any settled notion of my own very little thought brought me to agree with you fully. It is true Mat I was then led off into a train of thought and was regretting some things for which you are not to blame when you charged me with taking a place on the fence. What I was regretting is that too much of the little energy that I have used in life was given to the public. Travelling and politics required time and means that ought to have been applied differently. I renewed that train of thought after retiring that night and it was long before sleep came to dispel it. When I told you that the next few years of my life should it be prolonged would be a time of trial and you yielded to my strong desire to have you with me you seemed more than ever endeared to me. Although matters are not as I desire them at present with the blessings of providence and a proper use of time I look confidently to the future. My thoughts were turned to the law at a time when I desired something in which I could forget every thing else. Having undertaken it though under some disadvantages nothing short of Providential interference shall prevent me from giving it sufficient time and attention to test my powers of success. Pardon this digression. I Am writing my thoughts as they succeed each other without much regularity. Just as I hope to talk to you many a long hour. While I have the most profound respect for you there is with it an assurance that you will over look little errors.

Allow me before closing to thank you in all sincerity for your well timed enquiry about little Roxie. It let to a conversation that was to me exceedingly pleasant. It seemed the first time to me that any-one had entered into my feelings.

Capt Crawfords Company goes to day by way of sweet water to Knoxville. A vacancy occured and my brother Rufus was elected Lieutenant without opposition. You had the kindness to enquire whether he would meet me at Philadelphia on the 4th. If the Regiment remains at Knoxville till that time he will probably do so Let me put you a little on your guard. he is much younger than me and some people are silly enough to think him better looking. Dont you fall into that belief. I am sending him and Lieutenant Smith of the same company as a present to two young ladies in Madisonville.

I have written a much longer letter than is usual with me. You may be assured that a reply would be read with the very greatest interest But it is so uncertain a matter on account of irregularity in post office affairs these time that I shall not allow my self to be disappointed should none come before I start. At least I shall not attribute it to your failure. Hoping to see you soon for the present

Adieu My Dear Mat     D.W. Siler

Macon County Collections

1. Maggie Edmonston letter to Brothers B.B. and B.F., 14 Jul 1864. Edmonston and Kelly Families Collection, Western Carolina University, Cullowhee, NC.

2. D.H. Gettys letter to Mrs. A.H. Slagle, 24 Dec 1861. C.W. Slagle Collection. Hunter Library Digital Collection, Western Carolina University, Cullowhee, NC.

3. D.H. Gettys letter to his Brother, 27 Dec 1861. C.W. Slagle Collection. Hunter Library Digital Collection, Western Carolina University, Cullowhee, NC.

4. D.H. Gettys letter to D.W. Siler, 5 Jan 1862. C.W. Slagle Collection. Hunter Library Digital Collection, Western Carolina University, Cullowhee, NC.

5. D.W. Siler letter to Capt. Bell, 23 Jan 1862. C.W. Slagle Collection, Hunter Library Digital Collection, Western Carolina University, Cullowhee, NC.

6. David W. Siler letter to Mattie, 21 Mar 1862. C.W. Slagle Collection. Hunter Library Digital Collection, Western Carolina University, Cullowhee, NC.

7. David W. Siler letter to Mattie, 5 May 1862. C.W. Slagle Collection. Hunter Library Digital Collection, Western Carolina University, Cullowhee, NC.

# 9. MADISON COUNTY COLLECTIONS

## Governor's Papers: Zebulon Baird Vance
## and Governor's Letter Book:  Zebulon Baird Vance

The letters from these collections provide documentation for an event which shocked North Carolinians in its brutality and served to demonstrate the anger and suspicion that existed in the westernmost counties of the state toward those who remained loyal to the Union.  In the western border counties of Madison and Yancey, residents were divided in their support of the Union and the Confederacy. Tensions over disparate loyalties, a lack of effective local governance, and the ransacking of stockpiled salt stores culminated in an event known as the Shelton Laurel Massacre which took place in Madison County in January 1863.

Salt was a vital commodity in the mountains of North Carolina where it was used to preserve food and tan hides. The availability of salt could determine survival for those who depended upon it. Local governments held the responsibility for procuring and distributing salt, but large numbers of their citizens were away fighting the war and lawlessness prevailed. When Madison County Unionists in the Shelton Laurel Valley, referred to as "Tories" in western North Carolina, ransacked salt stores in the town of Marshall, a terrifying chain of events began. The home of Colonel Lawrence Allen, the commander of the 64th NC Infantry and a native of Madison County was raided while he was in Virginia. Confederate General Henry Heth, commander of the Department of East Tennessee ordered Lawrence Allen and James Keith to subdue the uprising in Madison County and to punish the looters. Twelve looters were killed, and Governor Vance sent word not to harm captured Unionists. Augustus S. Merrimon was sent to oversee the situation.

Lietutenant Colonel James A. Keith, a Madison County native, was sent by an unwell Allen to quell the uprising. Fifteen men were rounded up and two escaped. Thirteen were executed by firing squad, including a thirteen year old who begged for mercy and a fifteen year old. Several women were hanged by the neck and severely beaten to try to secure confessions about the whereabouts of their husbands and sons. The bodies were dumped in a trench.

The brutality of these events horrified Augustus Merrimon who sent a report to Governor Vance. The citizens of Madison County and the surrounding countryside were infuriated and general unrest and anger prevailed in the region. The massacre was reported in a variety of newspapers across the country and even in Europe. Governor Vance vowed he would " follow him [Keith] to the gates of hell, or hang him." For two years, Keith remained a fugitive before being captured by Union troops. He was indicted on thirteen counts of murder and served two years in prison being released by a general presidential pardon by Andrew Johnson. When he was freed, he moved to Arkansas fearing retribution from Madison county natives. Allen was suspended from active duty for six months. Heth received neither punishment nor censure.

The letters that follow outline the investigations which sought to unravel the the facts surrounding the incident.

## Augustus S. Merrimon to Gov. Zebulon B. Vance[1]

Asheville N.C.
Jany, 31st 1863
Governor;

The Arms ect. have at length reached Asheville and I have turned the whole over to Col. N.N. Young, in persueant of your instructions. I have forwarded this recp't to Maj. T. D. Hogg.

I learn that the Laurel expedition is about over. I can't give you any of the details of the affair. I suppose the proper officer will report to you. I learn that a number of prisoners were shot without any trial or hearing whatever. I hope this is not true, but if so, the partie guilty of so dark a crime should be punished. Humanity revolts at so savage a crime. Our Militia had nothing to do with what was done on Laurel. I am glad of this. It turns out that the Militia were not really needed. So I thought in the onset and advice our people, but they + Genl. Polk could not be satisfied without calling out the militia. Nothing new - All Well.

I Am Resp. Truly

A.S. Merrimon
Gov. Z. B. Vance

**Augustus S. Merrimon**

## Augustus S. Merrimon to Gov. Zebulon B. Vance[2]

Ashville N.C.
Feby 16th 1863

Governor;

Your letter of the 9th imit [?] is just received: - I beg to assure you that I shall at the next term of the court, prosecute rigorously, such of the prisoners, to whom you direct my attention as may be turned over to civil authorities.

The late expedition to Laurel, sent four prisoners to jail and no of them was admitted to bail on yesterday, by Judge Baily. I understand there are women to send. I have no knowledge of my own finding the shooting of several prisoners on Laurel. I have learned however from a most reliable source, that thirteen of them were killed, that some of them were not taken in arms but at their homes, that all the men shot, thirteen, if not more, were prisoners at the time they were shot, that they were taken off to a secluded cove or gorge in the mountains and there made to kneel down and were then shot. One man was badly and mortally shot in the bowels + while he was writhing in agony and praying to God for mercy, a soldier mercilessly + brutally shot him in the head with his pistol. Several women were whipped! This I learned from one who got his information from one of the guilty parties. I learned that all this was done by order of Col. James A. Keith! I know not what you intend doing with guilty parties, but I suggest, that they are all guilty of Murder. I do not suppose they had any order to do so barbarous a deed, but if they had, the order was said absolutely, no matter by whom issued.

Such savage and barbarous cruelty is without a parallel in this state and I hope in every other. I am gratified that you intend to take the matter in hand. I will, make such investigation as I can, but I have no means of compelling any one to disclose facts to me. It will not be difficult, I learn, to prove that the prisoners were killed.

I assure you that I will prosecute all persons who have committed criminal offences in this circuit, at the next term of the court, and in the mean time, I will do all in my power to suppress crime and violence. They are fearfully on the increase in this section of the state. A reprieve might be made that would as tarnish you. (I have done all I could in reference to the complaints made to you from Jackson and Cherokee Country.)

It is matter of regret to anyone who reflects properly, that the Legislature refused to restore the Courts. The civil arm is weak with one court. The bad men of the land, there and fore, that the day of judgment and execution for their crimes will never come.] The firm operation of the machinery of Courts is indispensable to a proper administration of the law. Allow me to say a word or two in behalf of a friend. Capt. James W. Ray of the 60th reg., Col. McDowell, wishes to resign his office furnish a substitute and be discharged from the army. He thinks, and is given to understand that his resignation will not be probably be received. Can you aid him? If so, he begs that you will. His family are afflicted. He lost his infant child a few weeks since.

Dr. Robt W. Cooper of Col McDowells Reg. wants to be appointed Ass. Surg. Have you any place you can give him? He says he can give good references etc. You have the means and I need not add a word as to his merit or demerits.

Hyman [John Hyman] has about sold the Spectator Press to the Armory here for $1400. [?] the money will be applied to the Bank note. Nothing new All weel


I am Yours Truly
A.S. Merrimon

His Excellency
Gov. Z. B. Vance
Raleigh, N.C.
A.S. Merrimon
Feby 16th 1863

**Governor Zebulon B. Vance**

## Augustus S. Merrimon to Gov. Zebulon B. Vance[3]

February 24, 1863, Ashville, N.C.,

Letter from A.S. Merrimon to Governor Vance
Asheville, N.C., February 24, 1863.

[Hon. Zebulon B. Vance:]

Governor:

In obedience to your directions so to do, I have made inquiries and
gathered facts such as I could in reference to the shooting of certain
prisoners in Laurel Creek, in Madison County. I have to report to you that I
learned that the militia troops had nothing to do with what was done in
Laurel. Thirteen prisoners, at least, were killed by order of Lieut. Col. J. A.
Keith. Most of them were taken at their homes, and none of them made
resistance when taken; perhaps some of them ran. After they were taken
prisoners the soldiers took them off to a secluded place, made them kneel
down, and shot them. They were buried in a trench dug for the purpose.
Some two weeks since their bodies were removed to a grave-yard. I learned
that probably 8 of the 13 killed were not in the company that robbed
Marshall and other places. I suppose they were shot on suspicion. I cannot
learn the names of the soldiers who shot them. Some of them shrank from
the barbarous and brutal transaction at first, but were compelled to act.
This is a list of the names of those killed: Elison King (desperate man); Jo
Woods (desperate man); Will Shelton, twenty years old (of Sipus); Aronnata
Shelton, fourteen years old (was not at Marshall); James Shelton (old Jim),
about fifty-six years old; James Shelton, jr., seventeen years old; David
Shelton, thirteen years old (was not in the raid); James Madcap, forty years
old; Rod Shelton (Stob Rod); David Shelton (brother of Stob Rod); Joseph
Cleandon, fifteen or sixteen years old; Helen Moore, twenty-five or thirty
years old; Wade Moore, twenty or twenty-five years old. It is said that those
whose names I have so marked did not go to Marshall. The prisoners were
captured on one Friday and killed the next Monday. Several women were
severely whipped and ropes were tied around their necks. It is said Col. L.
M. Allen was not in command and that Keith commanded. Four prisoners
are now in jail, sent here, as I learned, by order of General Davis. These are
Sipus Shelton, Isaac Shelton, William Morton, and David Shelton, son of
Sipus. I think the facts stated are about true. One thing is certain, 13
prisoners were shot without trial or any hearing whatever and in the most
cruel manner. I have no means of compelling witnesses to disclose facts to

me, and I do not know that I shall be able to make a fuller report to Your Excellency at any early day. I hope these facts will enable you to take such steps as will result in a more satisfactory development of the true state of the matter.

I am, &c., yours, truly,

A. S. Merrimon

## Gov. Zebulon B. Vance to Hon. James A Seddon, Secretary of War[4]

February 28, 1863, Raleigh, N.C.,
Governor Z. B. Vance to Secretary of War James A. Seddon

State Of North Carolina,
Executive Department.,
Raleigh, N.C., February 28, 1863.
Hon. James A. Seddon, Secretary of War:

Sir:

Some six months since a disturbance occurred in Madison County, North Carolina, near the Tennessee border, by some disloyal persons capturing the little county town and seizing a lot of salt and other plunder. An armed force was promptly sent from Knoxville, under command of General Davis, to suppress the insurrection, which was accomplished before the local militia could get there, though ordered out immediately. But in doing so a degree of cruelty and barbarity was displayed, shocking and outrageous in the extreme, on the part of Lieut. Col. J. A. Keith, Sixty-fourth North Carolina Troops, who seems to have been in command, and to have acted in this respect without orders from his superiors, so far as I can learn. I beg leave to ask you to read the inclosed letter (copy) from A. S. Merrimon, State's attorney for that judicial district, which you will see discloses a scene of horror disgraceful to civilization. I desire you to have proceedings instituted at once against this officer, who, if the half be true, is a disgrace to the service and to North Carolina. You may depend upon the respectability and fairness of Mr. Merrimon, who made an investigation officially by my order. I have also written General Davis.

Very respectfully, your obedient servant,
Z. B. Vance.

**James A. Seddon, Secretary of War**

## Gov. Zebulon B. Vance to Hon. James A Seddon, Secretary of War[5]

May 18, 1863, Raleigh N.C.,

Governor Z. B. Vance to Secretary of War James A. Seddon
Executive Department, Raleigh, May 18, 1863.
Hon. James A. Seddon, Secretary of War, Richmond, Va.

Sir:

I had the honor to request of you some time since an examination into the case of Lieut. Col. J. A. Keith, Sixty-fourth North Carolina Troops, charged with the murder of some unarmed prisoners and little boys during the recent troubles in the mountains of this State. I have heard by rumor only that he was brought before a court-martial and honorably acquitted by producing an order for his conduct from General Davis, commanding in East Tennessee. I have also been officially notified of his resignation. Will it be consistent with your sense of duty to furnish me a copy of the proceedings of the court-martial in his case? Murder is a crime against the common law in this State and he is now subject to that law.

Very respectfully, &c.,
Z. B. Vance

### Hon. James A Seddon, Secretary of War to Gov. Zebulon B. Vance[6]

Confederate States of America
War Department
Richmond, Va. May 23, 1863

His Excellency
Z B Vance
Gov. N.C.

Your letter of the 18th just has been rec'd. the resignation of Lt. Col. Keith was accepted at the office of the Ad. & Ins. General the 15 inst. No proceedings of a court Martial in his case have been rec'd. His resignation was accepted on the recommendation of Col. Palmer commanding the brigade & Maj Genl Maury - the examining board having [?] aganist his competency. The Adj. & Insp. Genl was not aware of the facts of the alleged murder, as applying to this officer at the time of his action on the resignation, where hving no reference to the facts in the papers before him.

In a communication to the department by Lt. Col. Keith, he claims that Br Genl Heth gave him a verbal order to this effect. I rec'd [?] no reports from you about your [?] at Laurel. I do not [?] to the trouble with any prisoners & the last one of them should be killed_ That he further to state, that he had been troubled with several prisoners from Laurel, N.C. and he did not want any man brought to Knoxville_

This statement is supported by the deposition [?] of a Dr. Thompson, & Keith [?] in his letter that he can prove it by another witness.

The communication of Keith & the disposition of Thompson were submitted to Br. Genl Heth for records - He says that he gave written instructions to Keith which he found in the books of the Dept. of E. Tenn._ he admits that he told Keith that those found in arms ought not be treated as enemies & in the event of our engagement with them to take no prisoners, as he considered that they had forfeited all such claims _ But he denines[?] in strong terms the making use of any remarks which would authorize maltreatment of prisoners who had been accept as such, as to women & children.

Very Respectfully
Yr Obit Svt
James A. Seddon
Secy of War

**General Henry Heth**

## Petition of Shelton Laurel Women of Madison County
## to Gov. Zebulon B. Vance[7]

Shelton Laurel

May the 29th 1863

State of North Carolina Madison County

We the undersigned do petition to the honerable governor of this state to have money propriated for us women to buy provisions for us being as we will bee bound to suffer on acount of troops eating up all our provisions and killing our men and property and destroying the country and if you will pleas to do so it will bee a kindness to us in so doing and we will kindly thank you with Respects

Judah Shelton
Nancy King
Martha Jane Shelton
Polly Shelton
Liney Norton
Marget Shelton
Sarah Shelton
Rachel Shelton
Emuline Riddle
Rody Hall

Som of those women is in prisoon and sum of them never had any men but all their property was destroyed.

## Sheriff S.G. Brigman, Madison County to Provost Marshal
## Col. Edward Hinks (Excerpt #1)[8]

September 18, 1867

Col: In compliance with your request endorsement Sept. 3, 1867 I have the honor to make the following report of James A. Keith – He is full six feet high, Dk hair, and very heavy black beard, generally wears his beard long,– weighs 180 to 185 lbs,–rather slow spoken but very intelligent and well posted on matters of history, etc.—was in the Mexican War and practicing physical while in this county. Age, about 43 or 45 and, while talking or interrogated, keeps one eye shut. The said James A. Keith was at one time a Col in the Rebel Army but was dismissed for robbery, murder, and a general plunder. He then organized a band of robbers and went about plundering & murdering on his own hood. He remained in the county (Madison Co) until about the time of the surrender, when he left and went to Greenville Dist., South Carolina, where he now lives.—Keith formerly lived in this County, in fact he has lived here all his life until he left about the [time of the] surrender. He bought the farm formerly owned by Col. L. M. Allen on South Tiger River 3 miles or 6 miles from Weavers old factory .— He bought this farm with property stolen from this country —.

His residence is 18 miles from Greenville C.H. North near the Spartanburg Dist. Line, not very far from the foot of Blue Ridge – Near a road leading from Henderson, N.C. to Spartanburg C. H., S. C.— Lives in a nice small white house [with] a portico in front, stables, and out houses below, stairway going up in center. It appears from the statement that the officer who made the search did not go near the directions, as this man Keith who he arrested lived in Pickens Dist., while James A. Keith lives near the Spartanburg line, the opposite direction. South Tiger River is very noted and he lives ¼ of a mile of said river. This same man Keith was seen but a few weeks ago lurking in this county and is well known and feared by every man in Western Carolina.

Keith has a wife and one or two small children, his wife's maiden name was Jones and lived in Tenn – Keith was [arrested?] one time before the war for forging a Bank Check.

Keith's Post Office is Travellers Rest.—I forwarded you last Mail affidavits of his guilt and Certificates of Clerks. I have capias, State warrants, and all manner of papers against Keith. He would likely be very easily arrested now, but soon he will commence his ramble of plunder.

If anything further is required of me you will advise me of the same.

I am Col Very Respectfully
Your Obdt Servant
S. G. Brigman
Sheriff of Madison Co., N.C.

### Sheriff S.G. Brigman, Madison County to Provost Marshal
### Col. Edward Hinks (Excerpt #2)[9]

September 18, 1867

I have the honor to forward affidavits of Several persons in regard to James A. Keith murdering several union men in this county. I can if you require send more than fifty affidavits of this kind. There are several true bills against him in the courts of this county for murder and one for arson for burning Thos. S. Denver's mills long after the surrender. The said James A. Keith . . . intended to burn and destroy every union man in the county – commencing on T. S. Denver, a leading union man.—Denver has again rebuild his mills at the cost of several thousand dollars. Keith has since been seen lurking about and has said they should not stand long. I have had capias and papers against him and have them now but he is [beyond?] our search. If Keith could be arrested and brought to the county there is sufficient charges against him to hang 500 men.

S.G. Brigman, Sheriff of Madison Co., N.C.

# NOTICE.

10

# $300 REWARD.

Broke jail, in Buncombe County, on the night of the twenty-first instant, the following named and described prisoners, viz: James A. Keith, D. L. Presley, and W. H. Walker.

Keith is about six feet high, dark complexion. gray or blue eyes, slim face, high forehead, prominent cheek-bones, black hair and beard, was unshaved at the time of escaping from prison, and is the rise of forty years of age. *once a little crossed*

Presley is about five feet ten inches high. swarthy complexion, light hair, blue eyes. downcast look, about twenty-two years of age, weighs about 150 pounds.

W. H. Walker is about five feet eight or ten inches high, dark complexion, dark-brown hair and rather inclined to be curly, blue eyes, is about thirty years of age. stoutly built, and weighs about 150 pounds.

I will give the above named reward of one hundred and fifty dollars for the delivery to me at Asheville. in the County of Buncombe, N. C., or confined in any jail within the State, of the above described persons, or fifty dollars for the delivery of either of them.

      **J. SUMNER**, Sheriff Buncombe Co.
Asheville, N. C., February 22, 1869.

In addition to the above reward I will give one hundred and fifty dollars for the delivery to me, or to the Sheriff, all of the above escaped prisoners, or fifty dollars for either of them.

        **T. K. DAVIS, Jailer.**

**Wanted poster for Lieutenant Colonel James A. Keith**

Madison County Collections

1. Augustus S. Merrimon letter to Gov. Zebulon Vance, 31 Jan 1863. Governors' Papers, Vance, 1863, NC Digital Collections. State Archives of North Carolina: Civil War Collection.

2. Augustus S. Merrimon letter to Gov. Zebulon Vance, 16 Feb 1863. Governors' Papers, Vance, 1863, NC Digital Collections. State Archives of North Carolina: Civil War Collection.

3. Augustus S. Merrimon letter to Gov. Zebulon Vance, 24 Feb 1863. Governors' Papers, Vance, 1863, NC Digital Collections. States Archives of North Carolina: Civil War Collection.

4. Gov. Zebulon Vance letter to James A. Seddon, 28 Feb 1863. Governors' Papers, Vance, 1863, NC Digital Collections. State Archives of North Carolina: Civil War Collection.

5. Gov. Zebulon Vance letter to James A. Seddon, 18 May 1863. Governors' Papers, Vance, 1863, NC Digital Collections. State Archives of North Carolina: Civil War Collection.

6. James A. Seddon, Sect'y of War, letter to Gov. Zebulon Vance, 23 May 1863. Governors' Letter Book, Vance, 1863, NC Digital Collections. State Archives of North Carolina: Civil War Collection.

7. Petition of Shelton Laurel Women to Gov. Zebulon Vance, 29 May 1863. Governors' Papers, Vance, 1863, NC Digital Collections. State Archives of North Carolina: Civil War Collection.

8. Sheriff S. G. Brigman, Madison County, NC letter #1 to Col. Edward W. Hinks, 18 Sep 1867. Governors' Papers, Worth, 1867, NC Digital Collections. State Archives of North Carolina: Civil War Collection.

9. Sheriff S. G. Brigman, Madison County, NC letter #2 to Col. Edward W. Hinks, 18 Sep 1867. Governors' Papers, Worth, 1867, NC Digital Collections. State Archives of North Carolina: Civil War Collection.

10. Reward poster for James A. Keith and others, 22 Feb 1869. Governors' Papers, Holden, 1869, NC Digital Collection. State Archives of North Carolina: Civil War Collection.

# 10. MCDOWELL COUNTY COLLECTIONS

## Zebulon Baird Vance (1824-1915) Papers

One of the letters from the Zebulon Baird Vance (1824-1915) Papers was written by a prominent citizen of western North Carolina with strong political connections. She writes to the Governor to ask for his protection from deserters. Born Catherine Wilson, she was the daughter of James and Rebecca Wilson of Burke County, North Carolina. She married planter and politician Samuel Price Carson on May 10, 1831. Carson served in the North Carolina General Assembly, North Carolina Senate, US House of Representatives, and as a delegate to the North Carolina Constitutional Convention in 1835. After moving to Texas in 1836, Carson was elected a member of the Convention of 1836 in which he signed the Texas Declaration of Independence and the Constitution of the Republic of Texas. He later served as a Texas Secretary of State. Samuel and Catherine Carson had a daughter, and they also adopted Carson's illegitimate daughter, Emily.

## Poteet-Dickson Letters, 1861-1902

The brother of Peter Poteet of Burke County, Francis Marion Poteet (1827-1902) was a miller who lived in the Dysartsville area of McDowell County. He was conscripted in 1863, serving as a private in Company A, 49th North Carolina Infantry. His wife was Martha Hendley Poteet (1826-1902). The Poteets had thirteen children. Francis and Martha Poteet both died in April 1902.

## Catherine Carson to Gov. Zebulon B. Vance[1]

Buck Creek July 8th 1864
Governor Vance

Dear Sir,

I take the liberty of asking you whether you can not process my son's discharge from the army that he may come home to protect me and his sister.

Since the late raid on Camp Vance there are great many deserters in the woods one of them George arrested last fall. he and two others have been seen near my house they are well armed and [uttered?] threats that they will burn my mill and others wise [ipefune?] me. I am in constant fear some great [infiny.] All the men in the neighborhood are here and no white on the place. I have no confidence in the negroes. I you can make some arrangements for my son to be at home a part of his time or if there is anything that I can do to be [soking] as to let me know it. There is no one here that can advise me.

I am confident every gentleman in the county would [sien a jelision?], my son George H Carson is a private in the 6 Cavalry recently commanded by Col Folk of stations near Kingston this state.

Most respectfully Governor Vance
Catherine Carson.

P.S. George left home of the 6 become his furlough to get a horse. I don't know how long he will be getting to kingston horseback.

CC

**Carson House built by Colonel John Carson. McDowell County, NC**

### Francis M. Poteet to Martha H. Poteet[2]

My Dear Wife and Children

I seat my self this morning to drop you afew lines to let you now that I am
well at this time hoping these lines may Reach your kind hands and find you
injoying the same Blessing  I Want you to send me sum tobaco I Rote to
Higgins and Sent him word to doo All that he could and I would pay him
Paid to send me sum tobacco and send me sum unions sum pork if you had
it and Bake Me sum cakes  you now what to send as Well as I can tell you
you dont now how bad that I want to see you and My littel Babes I had to
stand gard last night and I hav got the Trimbles so bad that I cant Hardly
Rite  I sent you A ring by Pery Walker that I Made  I Want you to take care
of hit till I come home  I Want to see it Again  My Dear Wife I want you to
hug and kiss to my littel Children for me and tell them that I told you to
Doo so for me and I will Doo any thing for you that you send word for me
to do if it bee your will for me to Doo it  I want you to Rest easy ABout
that that I Rote to you In the third letter for I never expect to doo so any
More as long as I live I have shed many ateare sence that time  I Rote to
you that if you would orgive me I think that the Lord will for give me  I
sent 15 Dollars By Pery Walker  I have forgot whether I Rote to you
whether H.H. Taylor was gon are not I want you to Read them juste A few
lines to littel Children Mary Bee good to your Mother and Doo all for me
that She tell you to Doo for I dont think that she will tell you more than
you can Doo  Thomas and Elvizs Bee goo boys and help your Mother  I
think more of her than every body Els in this World  May God bless and
save you all is my prayer for Christ sake  I want you to Rite soon when you
git this letter

Francis M. Poteet to his loving Wife M. A. E. Poteet

## Francis M. Poteet to Martha H. Poteet[3]

Kinston NC      Nov 23the 1863

My Dear Wife and Children

I Received your kind & loving letter  it giv me great satisfaction and I was
mad too  I think it tis hard that you hav to giv that place up after sowing
your Wheat  I want you to tell Bill if he hant sent you that wheat that I want
him to send it bushel &  tobe [Dish fod?]  you Rote to me to git aferlow [a
furlough] if I could  I went to Kinston to day to see the Colonel and he
wasant at home  I dont now whether I will git it are not  if I dont I want
you to do the best you can till I git home and then I will help you  I want
you to tell Joseph Landis to pay you for them coffins  if he asks you what
you charge you can tell him if he will let you have wheat at one Dollar per
bushel that he can give you 6 bushel  if he dont you can tell him to pay you
$16 Dollars  you can tell him that you want the wheat  what did higgins giv
you for them berals  I dident hav nothing for My breakfirst only Corn Bred
and I went over to Kinston and I seed sum Crackers and I give fifty cents
for six about as big as a dollar  it seems like it will take all that I can make
hear to git sumthing to Eat and to git paper and tobacco and invelips  I had
to give thirty cents for this paper that I Rote this letter on and then I have
to pay from 25 to thirty cents per garment and it takes about all that I git
your letter you Rote the 19 I got it the 22  that is the first letter that I have
got in two weeks  I thought that you had for got me but I dont think you
have  you Rote to me that you had got my coat and you wanted to now
what I had done With my hat  I swated with higgins I could not git nary
other hat and I had to lay on it and wallow over it so I thought that I mites
swell let him have it as any way you Will think hard of me for that but I
Dont want you to think hard of me I could not take care of it  you Rote to
me that Higgins said that he would send the papers By Litel  I have got out
of hart that  I ever Will git home any more till this War ends  I am hear and
you are there so we are many Miles A part we bee but if I live till christmas
I think if God will let me live that long that I will git closter home  I trust in
God for every thing  if I had of bin at home when Bill Rented you out of
house and home I think that I would of heart him and I Dont now but
what I will yet but I ought to pray for him and any other man that does as
he does  the Bible teaches us to pray for our inmas [enemies] but it is hard
to pray for any Speclator [Speculator: one who drove up prices on
desperately needed goods] when tha doo so but I pray God to for give him
You Rote to me that higgins would Come down hear when he got his
Wheat sown  I Dont think that he has any Ida of it  may God help him to
think of my Wife and littel Children and Doo all he can  if I can come home

I dont want him to bee always about it  we had preachen hear twist sunday
But I would of been mutch glader to of bin at home to of went to  with you
I want you to Rite every week if it takes all that I make  I would rather see
you than to have one bushel of gold dust  it would give me more satsfaction
than all the gold that has bin dug out of Brachet town  I dont know what to
doo if I was to come home and then tha catch me then I would have to go
back but I think that I will try it sumtime if I live tell mother and sister that
I am tolerable well at this time hoping that she may be well  this is the
levlest contry that I ever saw it tis as leval as your garden tha ant a hill that
can be seen about hear  I had to go in Dres perade Just now and had to
finish my letter after wards  it tis nearly dark and I must come to A close by
saying that I Remain your loving husband until Death May God Bless and
save you all is my prayer

FM Poteet to his loving Wife and Children
kis my litel babes for Me my loving Wife M. A. E. Poteet

## Martha H. Poteet to Francis M. Poteet[4]

N C Mcdowell County   1864
thursday  January the 7

My Dear husband

I now seat my self to write you a few lines to let you know we are not well
the children is sick with bad colds and I haint seen a well day since you left
I have had a very bad head ache ever sens last Sunday but I do hope and
pray this will find you in good health the Raleigh gard never come back no
moor  I wish you could hav staid with me  Mr Walker and Johnathan kiled
my hogs the day after you left  I cant get the William house he is a going to
move to it and I dont know what to do  Bill Cowen come hear a teusday
and told me to get out as soon as I could and what I am to do I dont know
one of the sheep is at Baty Grasons  I hav got one at home and I got the
cows home last teusday Thomas found them at Johnathan Taylors  you
thought it was cold when you was hear but it was nothing the 1 & 2 days of
this Month was the coldest I ever felt and it much warmer yet I dont
believe we hav had but two clear days sins you left Pery Walker sed you had
Washs gloves blanket and to send them to him I want you to tell him if he
was as willing for other people to hav there oune as he was for Wash to hav
his I would got my ring in the place of some one els  he talked like you had
stold the Blanket and gloves I want you to talk to the captain and know if
they cant put me out if they cant I wont leav  you can tell him how it is  if I
hav to moove I will sell the Mar and Cows and live while the corn and meat
last for I dont see how I am to get along with no one to help me  I hav to
pay tax on the cows I want to know what they don with you for runing
away  the men about hear says you will hav to come home in Companys
before peace will be mad and they say they wish you all would come and
says if the war dont stop the people will perish  they are enroling them from
18 to 55 and what are we to do if you all dont come home  O my dear
husband you dont know how lonsom I am sins you left  I dread to see
Night come O I do hope and pray that the Lord will spar our lives to see
each other in peace Once moor  O Lord be with my dear husband and
bless him for I cant be with him O Francis it dos seem like it will kill me to
be parted from you with no one to protect me and your little helpless
children I pray the Lord to save your sole and body fom harm if I never see
you no moor  I want you to write soon  I am so cold I must quit May the
Lord bless and save you is my prayer for Christ sake

Martha A. E. Poteet to my loving husband Francis M. Poteet
farwell my love till we meet again

## Martha H. Poteet to Francis M. Poteet[5]

N C  Mc dowell Co thursday
January 21 1864

My Dear husband

I recieved your kind letter last satturday and I was glad to hear that you was
well  I cant write we are all well we all hav bad colds  I hav had a pain in my
head three weeks and the baby is sick and I dont think it will live long but I
do hope this May Reach your kind hands and find you well  I would write
you some about My self but I cant let evry Man read what I would be
willing for you to read you want to know about the hogs I got Mr Walker
and Johnathan the next day to kill them I dont know about Ashville  John
Cowen and others was detailed to hall their provision back out of the way
of the yankeys and they say the yankeys can come hear in a day and a half
John Carson and Ranz Mitchel and his brother is going about taking up
paroled men and men with furlows  they taken John Waren last Teusday
and put him in Jail And Al Taylor but let him loos a few days  the men fom
18 to 50 has to go to the Armey in a short time and the Men fom 16 to 60
has to be home gard and negres to be [gentle?] men  this is three letters I
hav wrote you I went to the cross Roads last Saturday and got two dollars
worth salt and Sunday Night some body stold about half of it and about a
half bushel of beans and they hav taken a heap of my corn what I am to do
I dont know I thought wen a man went back with with in themselves they
did not put them in the gard house but George Taylor told he tuck you up
and is to get thirty Dollars of your wages and I expect that is the of you
being punished it is Just one Month today sins our little son died and I dont
think they ought to blame you for coming home to see him Die but I do
hope that God will be with you and bless you and save fom all harm  I hope
the war will stop and you can come home in peace Sally Hendley had a fine
son thursday lat  I want you to do the best you can and serve the Lord and
if we Meet no moor in this world Ihope we will Meet in heaven to part to
moor  May the Lord bless save you is my prayer for Christ sake  write soon
and often  farwell

Martha A. E. Poteet to her loving husband Francis M. Poteet
God bless you my husband

## Martha H. Poteet to Francis M. Poteet[6]

tell grise I seen Nancy last sunday  she is well

N C Mcdowell Co 1864
thursday  Feb the 4

My Dear husband

I recieved your kind and loving letter last saturday and was glad to hear fom
you and hear you was well but sory to hear sunday that you was not well
we are not well  they nearly all hav had sore throats  I aint well my self but I
do hope and pray that when these few lines reaches your kind hands it will
find you well  I shal be uneasy till I hear fom you  if I could I would come
and see you  I sent you somthing to eat by Marion Higins five pies and five
ginger Cakes one doz unions two custerds 1 ham of Meat and three twists
of tobaco  I toted it to the X roads in my lap  if you get it I wont mind
nothing that I don  I am willing to do any for you that I can  You wrote for
me to stay hear  Bill Cowen says if I stay in the house I shant work the
ground that I shant as much as hav the garden  I hav walked my self down
this week trying to get a place and hav got non  me and my children are
bound to perish  all the honest men is gone and a set of speckalating
dogs[Speculators were those who drove up prices on desperately needed
goods] is left to press the lives out of the poor Women and children while
the soldiers is standing as a wall between them and the enemy  they are
standing between them and there wives to snatch evry thing they can get  I
think there ought to be astop put to it  if it aint we all will be bound to
perrish  I am in a great deal of trouble  Doctor Young charged me three
dollars in gold or silver or thirty dollars in confederate for coming to see
Alvis one time and george Taylor to hav thirty dollars for his kindness leting
you rid to the head of the road  he ought to be double quicked to the armey
if I was a man I would kill him  Bill Cowen had go to Richmond  he sed he
would give 12 hundred penny weights of gold to get off  Young Burt
Higgins died last sunday there has bin several deaths in the last two or three
weeks  your Aunt Barbry died last sunday week  your Mother is in Burk
[Burke County]yet  I want you when you write to write to me and not to
them that dont thank you for it  I thought you had better sens that any body
that dont car for me nor you  I want it to be the last  I hav had but two little
scraps of letters yet and I hav wrote five  I will send you apeace of paper I
told you when you left I was left to the Mercy of the people  there is about
as much mercy shown me as a dog would show apeace of meat but I hope
it wont always be so  I do hope that peace will be made and you can come
home  O that God will spar your Life to get home and bless you with

health and shield you fom all harm is the prayer of your disstressed Wife  I
want you to do the best you can  I hope they wont punish you all ways I
dont think they ought  you did not stay at but 8 days and then went back
but if God is with you you need not fear what Man can do  I dont expect to
see you any moor in this world but I want to meet you in heaven  I must
close farwell Francis My dear  May we meet again in peace

M. A. E. Poteet to her Loving husband F. M. Poteet
God bless you

## Francis M. Poteet to Martha H. Poteet[7]

Weldon NC
February 8th 1864

My Dear Wife and [little children?]

I[part of page missing at fold]have had the head ache about 18 days and
nights I have got better I Received your kind letter and was glad to hear
from you I Received the box you sent but all the pies and custerds was
spoilt I never tasted them I was sory of that for I would Rather had them
than any thing that you sent me but I was glad to git the other I hope that
you can git aplase that you can make your suport on I dont think that the
lord will not let you parish hope that you can git sumthing to live on while
others has it tis hard times every where but cant help the hard times I was
glad of the tobaco that you sent me but tho I cant Rite mutch I [torn] hear
tha is so mutch [torn] think of any thing but I am in hops that you can Read
it you dident Rite any thing about the baby I hope that she is well I am
glad that you sent me sum paper to Rite you a letter I hope that the agrd
[guard] will let this letter come to you and my littel Children I hope and
pray to god that tha will let this letter come I hope these lines may I have
Received 4 letters from you I hant Rote you two [hope?]ping you all well it
tis with God that we [torn] live and breath when he [torn] things will be
done I have to pray to my god every day that tha will be peace in this land
once more I want you to Rite to me about Henry and Sydney my brothers
whether tha are well are not are whether tha got wounded are not I seen
Henry when I was at the head of the Road he looked very bad and he
looked like he was very near don for this world I hant heard from them
sence I have bin hear you Rote that Will Cowen would not let you have the
land I dont now what to think of him only that he is one of the worst
spelator [Speculators were those who drove up prices on desperately
needed goods]in this world may god bless and save you and my littel
Children god is abel [torn] thing but we have to [torn] is Redy when every
thing gits Right them he will deliver us and not before I must close by
saying that I Remain your loving husband until death

F. M. Poteet to his loving Wife M. A. E. Poteet

gard please send this to my Wife
if you pleas

## Martha H. Poteet to Francis M. Poteet[8]

N C  Mcdowell Co 1864      Feb thursday the 18

My Dear husband

 I seat my self to write you afew lines to let you know that we are only
tolerable well I am a little better than I hav bin  My baby dont see a well day
but I do hope and pray that these few lines may reach your kind hands and
find you in good health for I am uneasy about you  I haint heard from you
in most four Weeks and it [?] [longer?] [line obscured by fold] a year hav
you forgot me or cant you write  I would like to know what is the reason
you dont write  the last I heard fom you you was sick  I would be very glad
to hear from you I feel very lonly and troubled to think I cant hear fom you
I want you to tell me what to do about giving apart of the crop to Henrietta
she says she is going to take the sow and pigs  I want to know if they aint
yours and write to me what to do about it  she said that you was not to hav
her for the one that you killed last winter  I think she is acting very mean to
do as she is doing to try to sell the sow and tell a lie and say they are hers
she sed she would hav them or kill them in the woods write what for me to
do about them  I want your word to show Joseph Landis was Married last
Saturday Night to Jeanna[?] Coopper a daughter of Bill Coopper  what kin
is he to Susy Coopper  we hav had the prettyest weather for the last five or
six weeks  it was like corn planting time but it is very Cold now  I think it
will snow we had snow last Monday but it Melted off  they are furlowing
fom the 22 regiment  E. Neal Barny Brackett and son Hufstuttle  Overton
West Grason Dickson has all bin home lately and John Cowen and
johnathan Taylor is at home half of there times  if you could get to come as
they do it would be a great help to Me  the yankeys got Soloman Barns
they say that this state will go in to the union and South Carolina is going as
soon this state dos the quarter Marsters [quartermasters were responsible
for securing provisions for the Army] is to be round next week to get all the
dry Cattle I dont see what on Earth we will do there aint corn to do till
Harvest and Wheat dont look like it will be any acount  for My part I dont
know what I am to do  I do wish and pray peace would be Made so that
you could come home to help Me Make support for our little children  I
want you to get a furlow by the 12th of May and Come Home to take care
of me I want you to do the best you can and serve the Lord and pray for
me and I will for you My heart and eyes is so full I cant hardly write  write
soon and often  I want to know if you got the box of things I sent by
Marion Higgins  May the Lord bless and save you is the prayer of your
disolate Wife farwell dear        Martha A. E. Poteet to her loving husband
Francis M. Poteet  remember me  god bless you My dear husband

## Francis M. Poteet to Martha H. Poteet[9]

Weldon NC
Feb 23the 1864

My Dear Wife and Children

I seat my self down this morning to drop you afew lines to let you now that I am well at this time hoping these lines may Reach your kind hands and find you injoy the same blessings  you Rote to me about the hogs  you tell them that tha are mine and tha are the dearest hogs that I ever got  you can tell Joseph Landis that any body that trobels them if I live to git home tha will suffer for them  you can tell Henritta that I mantained her when no other person would not and she had better doo Right that she may need help again and she might not git hit  tell her that she can have one of the pigs if she want it  I hope that God will bless you all  I want you to send me some more unions & tobacco and one lite lofe of corn bread if you can  the box that you sent me the pies and the tarts was spoiled  I got it the 7 of this month  Send me sum dride fruit if you can  I am in the gard house yet  I got your letter yesterday and was glad to hear from you and glad to hear that you was better  may God bless and save you is my prayer for Christ Sake
farewell My loving Wife

F. M. Poteet to his loving Wife M. A. E. Poteet

## Martha H. Poteet to Francis M. Poteet[10]

Mcdowell Co N C
April the 7 1864

My Dear husband

I seat My self this Morning to write you a few lines to let you know that we
are only tolerable well  we have very bad colds  I am so hoars that I cant
hardly talk and sis has had the Croup this week but I do hope these few
lines May reach your kind hands and find you well  I haint had no letter in
two Weeks  I would be glad to hear from you  I have got 2 bushels of sweet
potatoes and planted them  I planted 7 & 33 hills and I have to pay 100
[$1.00?] dollar per bushel  I haint planted Corn yet I want to plant next
Week if it dont rain last week somebody stold two of Allens horses and left
two old poor no count ones in there place and last Monday Night some
body stold 20 peices of bacon from him [besides?] the rest Joints last
Monday all the Men was ordered from Camp Vance to Ashville  they say
that the yankeys can come here at any time they please but they dont want
to come for there aint any thing to come for but a parcel of half perished
women and children  half of my time I dont have nothing for breakfast but
Cornbread and bran coffee  it is hard living but I hope it wont be so all
ways  I cant buy one mouth full of nothing to eat and thread sells for 3
penny weights of gold for a bunch and I cant get non  I hav fifty cents in
confederate  salt is one dollar a pound  they have quit keeping goverment
salt at the X roads  I give three dollars old state Money and two confederate
dollars for 8 lbs of salt how I am to get along God knows I don't  they are
looking for Marion Higgins home and I will try and get him to take you
somthing to eat  I am sorry I could not send you somthing before now but
you know that I would if I could  I have had a many a tear about it  I aint
able to bring it My self and I cant get no erson to take you somthing to eate
and if I was able to come I dont think it is aplace fit for women except it be
in case of sickness then I would come if I had to beg my way to you I want
to see you very much but I cant come to you but I hope that your head man
will let you come to me before long you must do the best you can  put your
trust in God  fear not what man can do  they can but kill the body but fear
God that can kill both sole and body  pray for me dear husband that I [my
life?] may be spard to to take care of my little children for I am in a helpless
condition  no one to look too for help but God alone but he is able to save
all them that put there trust in him  I trust in him and I try to pray for you
my self and our little children and for peace so that you all can come to
your friends but if I see you no moor in this world I hope to meet you in
heaven where we will be separated no moor but if it is Gods will I would be

glad to see you in this life
May God bless you and save from harm and danger is my prayer

M. A. E. Poteet to her loving husband F. M. Poteet
farwell my dear Francis

please gard give this to my husband

## Francis M. Poteet and Thomas M. Hendley to Martha H. Poteet[11]

Richmond, Va.    May 4th 1864

My Dear Wife

This leaves me well and I hope it will find you and the children in good
health  I left Weldon yesterday and arivd hear this morning  I have writ
three letters Since I Recevd one from you  the last I Recevd from you was
dated April the 7 I do not know how long I will be kept hear or what will
be don with me but I may be Sent to Salisbury I would like to See you all
but I do not know when I will hav that prevelage but I hope it will not be
long before pease is made and that we will all get home once more I Seen
Washing Mooney this moning but I did not get to Speake to him  I also
found your Brother Thomas hear  he is as well as usual and will write you
afew lines in this letter I want you to write to me as Soon as you get this
letter and write me all of the news and how the people are getting on let me
know how your Wheat looks and what is the prospect of the Wheat crop
janerally and if the fruit is killed By the late cold - tell Comadore Grist
family that he is hear and as well as usual  I know nothing moore to writ at
this time  I mearly write to let you know whare I am  write as soon as you
Recieve this
Yours Truly
F.M. Poteet

Dirict Your letter
F.M. Poteet
Care of Capt Richerson
Castle Thunder
Richmond Va.
Room no. 8

My Dear Sister

I will write you afew lines in Franks letter I am as well as usual and I hope
you and the children are well I was very gald [glad] to See frank He look as
well as I ever Seen him I hope we will stay together till we are permitted to
come home and I do pray it will not be long before this Cruel war is ended
and that we will all git home to our family and friends I know nothing new
to writ you  times are very hard hear tell Sally that I am [?]and that I am
expecting a letter from her this week and that I will writ to her [?]
Your loving Brother    T.M. Hendley

## Francis M. Poteet to Martha H. Poteet[12]

God bless and Save
you and our littel children

Camp Burmuda Hundred Va
May 31th 1864

Dear Wife and Children

I Seat my self Down to Drop you afew lines to let you now that I am well at
this time hoping that these lines may Reach your kind hands and find you
all [?] Doing Well  I Received your kind letter that was dated the 20 and was
glad to hear from you and hear tha you was well  I got the plat of hear that
you Sent [plait of hair] me I left your Brother in Richmond Monday
Eavning  he hated to See me start  I had to get to My Redgment and he had
to go to his  When I got to my Redgment I got that other letter that had the
plat of hear  in hit  you Rote that you had got your corn over the first time
I was glad to hear that you was getting Along as  you are  I have praid for
you and my littel children all the time and praid that you might have A good
time  I loud that when I seen the back of your letter that you had got
through but when I Red it I found out that you hadant  we are in line of
battel Now and [E?] Whisant was [Sh?ed] yesterday and I met the men
taking him out to the amanabus [omnibus] to take him to the horse pittel
[hospital]  I want you to pray for me and tell all of my Friends to pray for
me to Spear my life to git home once more to See you all again in this life  I
doo hope and pray to god to Spear my life to git home once more to See
you all and find you all well  G.W. Mooney is with me  he Said that he
would Rite  I have bin out of prison 22 days I think that your brother was
the gladest to See me When I got in prison that I must close by Saying Rite
Soon

F.M. Poteet to his loving Wife M.A.E. Poteet

## Martha H. Poteet to Francis M. Poteet[13]

June the 16 1864

My Dear husband

I seat My self this evening to write you a few lines to let you know how we are Some of us is not well me nd Thomas Francis Emer Susannah Amy Jane has the bowell complaint I aint Much sick but I do hope these few lines May Reach your kind hands and find you in good health My corn looks very well Thomas will finish plowing it the second time today we hav this side the Creek to hoe My Neighbours says that if nothing happens I will Make a heap of Corn the sweet potatoes is very prety and the irish potatoes is the pretyest I ever seen I hav a mess today I wish you was hear to eat some with me I would be so glad I would not know how to behave I hav to live very hard I haint nothing Much to eat but bread and not Much of that if you was hear I would not hav to live so hard nor I woudent hav to work when I was not able My baby will be 4 weeks old Saturday Night she was born the 21 of May write to Me what to name her I had the best time I ever had and I hav bin the stoutest ever sens I haint lay in bed in day time in two Weeks today I thank the Lord that he has answerd your prayers and mine beyon what I could expected but he has all power I feel very thankfull that it is as well with you as what it is I hope that God will bless us to be spared to rais our children your Mother is well her and Jemima Come to see me yesterday Grason Dickson run away and got to Camp Vance and had to go back I dont want you to vote for vance vote for Holden vance is to be in Marion next Monday to speak James Neal has bought 500 bushels of corn for this County but it haint come yet and he says that when they eat it they may die and go to hell Louis Walker and Tery Walker is at home wounded your Mother says tell you howdy for her and the children sends you howdy and tell you that they hav to work very hard and wishes you was hear to help them [?] this evening I would like to hear from you to know if you hav got hurt I am very uneasy about you I do hope and pray that God will shield you from all harm and danger and spar your life to come home to me and your little children I know that you want to see your sweet little baby I would be very glad to see you if I could but I cant nor I dont know whether I ever will or not God knows I dont you dont know what a hard time I hav I am ruined if you dont never come home I cant work another year as hard as I hav this if the children was not as good as they are I dont know what I would do the Lord has blessed us and I hope he will continue to bless us while we are separated and bring us together agin in this life pray for us my Dear that we dont perish thread is 100 dollars Cotten is two dollars apound I dont know what I am to do but

I will do the best I can and trust in God for help  all of our help comes from him write to me soon  wen I can hear fom you and hear that you are well it dos me a heap of good  May the lord bless and save you is the prayer of your desolate Wife  farwell my Dear husband

M. A. E. Poteet to her loving husband F. M. Poteet   God bless and save you

the sise of the babys hand

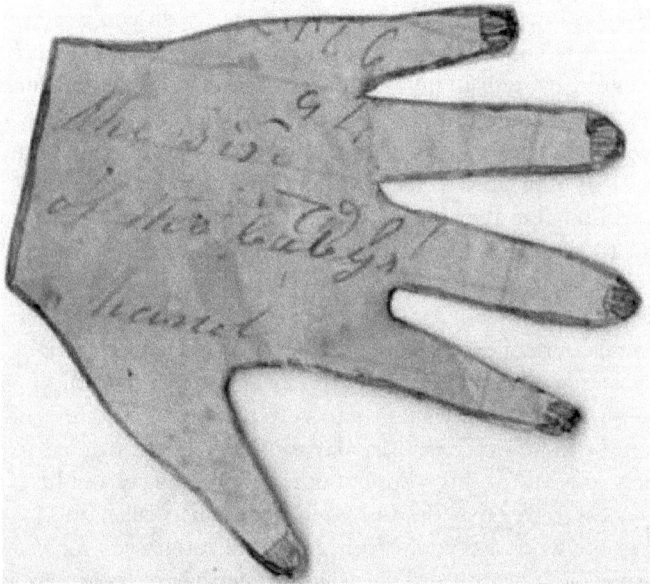

## Martha H. Poteet to Francis M. Poteet[14]

Remember me in love and I
will you  Farewell dear Francis

June the 16 1864

Dear husband

I cant get no person to cut my wheat  the men says that they dont know
what will be don with the wheat for there aint men to cut it and if I dont
get Mine cut me and the children will be bound to suffer  I would like for
you to show this to your Capt and tell him if he pleases to let you come
home a few days the first of July to take Care of it for me  I have about 8
bushels sowed and no person to cut a straw of it  it rains so much that we
cant get to work the corn scearsley and the Mare has had the distemper and
scurvey but is better now I had her bled and I want to know what to do
with hink  Must I kill her this fall  I hav tried to swap her for a cow that
gives Milk and I cant  I dont get a drop of milk and I haint got but a few
pounds of meat times is very hard hear and I am afraid that the worst haint
come if this Cruil war dont stop  I would rather know that peace was Made
than to own Mcdowell County  it would be moor satisfaction I haint got no
money I sent 30 dollars off by Higgins to get new money and I haint got it
yet and no person haint paid me that was owing you and I dont know what
I will do  Come if they will let you
M.A.E. Poteet to F.M. Poteet god bless you

Privit F.M. Poteet Co.
A 49 Redgment N C

to M.A.E. Poteet
Dysartsville Po
McDowell County N C

## Martha H. Poteet to Francis M. Poteet[15]

Mc dowell Co Oct 6th 1864

Dear husband

I seat My self this Morning to write you a few lines to let you know that we are not well  I aint well My self and the children aint well  Francis Emmer is very low with the flux and the baby is very sick  I dont know what ails her  I recieved your kind letter that was dated the 25 of Sept last Saturday and was glad to hear from you once moor and hear that you was still alive  I hav wrote evry week but one  I sent a letter by Louis Walker and one by Herksy and paper to write two letters  the Assosiation has past over  there was 14 or 15 preachers there  your couisen bob Moody was there  he preached on sunday  it rained so Much that they dident hav Much of a assosiation  it has raind nearly all the time for 3 weeks  it is raining now  there is a power of fodder lost  I hav saved the crib full of fodder  I dont know what I am to do some boddy is stealing the corn out of the field and stealing My sweet potatoes after I Me and the children has worked so hard to Make somthing to live on  I want you to keep trying to get a furlow  tell them that your family is down with the Measels and flux and there aint nobody to gather the corn and I will hav to moove and they Must let you come and Moove Me  I haint got no peas & beans picked yet and if we dont get well & it dont quit raining I wont save seed  I hav had to go in the rain so Much  I so much to do that I dont see a well day  My grief and troubles is Moor than I can bear  if you dont get to come I dont know what will become of Me and the children my pen is so bad I cant write and My heart is so full I cant think of what I ought to  oh God have Mercy on My husband and children and my self  Spar our lives to meet in this world once moor  the 12th day of this Month is a year that we hav bin parted and it seems all most a life time do the best you can  keep out of them fights as much as you can and if you can get a furlow come home if you plase but if you cant get a furlow you cant do me any good to come but it would do me harm  you know if I was able and the children was well I would come to see you if I had to beg My way to you  I would tell you Moor that I can write  some times I feel like you will get to come home  the one that told your forchen says that you will get to come before you get well but if they Miss it as bad as you sed they did about the other it wont be the truth  Brother Thomas is alittle better  I wish you could bring some of that tobacco home with you  I think it is very Mean that they dont let you come  if you was a rich mans son you could come  Marion Higgins has bin at home a Month and he looks well  Thomas Satterwhit & Willie Grason has ben at home on a sick furlow  if you dont get home soon I will send you a pare of socks by bob Mooney friday

Morning 7th the children aint no better I think susannah George Pinkney is taking flux Mary [?las?] is very low with the flux the flux followers the Measels I hope when I write again they will be better I hop the Lord will bless you and Shield you from harm and danger and spar your life to get home soon

M. A. E. Poteet to My husband F. M. Poteet

Oct 7, 1864

I expect it was a tooth Canker that the baby had come by her not cutting her teeth sooner it come from her jawbone and morterfied as it went if I had of had some of your water I could cured her but I couldent get it and she is ded and gone to heaven out this troublesom world in heaven with her brother and Jesus her savour but I am sory to give her up oh if I could see her one time moor but I cant now but I will some time and I hope we will part no moor and I will see my dear little son and all my friends in heaven I hope and if we meet no moor on Earth I want to meet you in heaven but I do hope and pray to God that we will be spared to see ech other in this world again oh Lord spar the life of my own dear husband to return to me again soon shield him from all harm and danger give him somthing to eat and ware and bless him abundently I want you to write soon if you please will you need any moor socks this winter let me know I will close

M A E Poteet to my husband F M Poteet
farewell

God bless and save you dear Francis

## Francis M. Poteet to Martha H. Poteet[16]

Oct. 23the 1864

PetersBurg, VA.

Dear Wife and children

I Seat my Self this morning to Rite you afew lines to inform you that I am well at this time hoping that these lines may Reach your kind hands and find you in good health you Rote to me that all of the Children was sick  I hope and pray to god that tha may git well again and live till I git to come home and see them once more in this life I think it would bee more satisfaction to me to see you all than any thing that ever I saw  you Rote for me to Rite to you about the mare I dont now what to say about it  I want you to doo the best that you now how if you think that it tis the best I want you to sell her  you Rote that you dident think that you had and Rased Corn to fatain [fatten] your hogs and winter the cowes  I hope and pray to god that you have Received that other letter that I Rote to you  I Rote for you to go and see Jacob Moore  I think that he will let you have that plase  Dear Wife it seems like it will Breake my heart when I open one of your letters  I cant keep from crying you Rote that Mrs. Walker was dead  I was sorrow to hear of that but we all have to die  I heard that Mrs Deal was ded I dident hear what was the matter whither I still want you to send me sumthing to eat if you can you know what to send as well as I now what to tell you you Rote that all of the Taylors was at home and all of the Prices  I think that tha will have to come yet  I want you to Rite as soon as this comes to hand I hope that the lord will bless you all

F.M. Poteet to M.A.E. Poteet

Fare well Martha for this time god bless and save you is the prayer of your loving husband

## Martha H. Poteet to Francis M. Poteet[17]

N C  Mcdowell Co
Nov 24th 1864

Dear husband

I Seat My self this eavning to write you a few lines to let you know that we
are still in the land of the living I aint very well  the children is well
excepting bad colds but I do hope these few lines will Reach your kind
hands and find you well I hav got my corn gathered and wheat Sowed  I
sowed the upper field in wheat the Burk Melisha [Burke Militia} is out this
week after [Burke County militia]deserters they come up with the Johnsons
and others and fired on them and they returned the fire and after firing a
bout [?] rounds the deserters run in the time of the fray Sydney Poteet got
badly wounded in his arm  the ball went in below his Elbow went through
his Elbow and the ball lodged in his arm above his Elbow  it was a large
minie ball they got three deserters and loud they killed some they seen them
fall yesterday they went to Henry Deales hunting the Johnson and give hally
a malling for his sassy talk times is very bad here now nbodys life is worth a
days perches and I dont look for this war to stop for 4 years yet without the
soldiers all comes home  they will take Thomas from me next summer and
then what will I do  George Taylor was after him a few weeks ago  brother
Thomas has to start back next teusday  old Mr [Powell?] is dead  Johnathan
Walker is in georgia in the gard house  the weather is very cold hear now I
sent you a box of provision  I recon it wasent good  you wrote to your
Mother and mima to send you a box of provision I hope they will send you
somthing good and plenty of it  I sent as good as I could get and the baby
died in the time I was fixing it and you all so wrote to your mamy to not let
your children suffer if we dont keep our selves from suffering with out help
from any plase we will perish  I think it makes me look very small for you
to write the like to her when you know that she wont help them  just for
her to tell about all the country what you wrote her like you had moor
confidens in her raising your children than me  she hardly ever gives them
an apple to eat much less to keep them from suffering  the last apple she
gave to me I sent it to you I was all ways one that wasent much cared for
my friends are few and fare between  God is My friend and helper and his
help is worth evry bodys els I haint had no letter sens the 31 of oct I dident
write last week I dident fell lik writing  if the war dont stop there will be
moor children that will perish besids yourn  I hav don all the work I could
and when I do all I can I cant do no moor  if I could make Money I could
by corn at Hemphills for 6 dollars a bushels before spring  it will be 20
dollars abushel  I dont see no sattisfactison  if I could I would come and see

you but I cant come  some times I feel like I cant stand it no longer but hav to put up with it and do the best I can  it has ben a long time sense I hav seen you and I dont expect I will see you soon but I hope the Lord will be with you if I cant and bless and save you and shield you from all harm and danger and spare you life to return home in pece soon I will hav to quit my pen has got mad and wont write and I am very cold  the children says to tell par howdy  I must close

M. A. E. Poteet to her loving husband F M Poteet may the Lord bless and save you farewell Francis

**Francis M. Poteet to Martha H. Poteet**[18]

Peters Burg V.A.
December 3th 1864

My Dear Wife and children

I Seat my self this morning to Rite you afew lines to let you now that I am
still in the land of the living yet  I am well and I hope and pray to god that
these few lines May Reach your kind hands and find you all Well  I
cant Rite without crying  it seems to me that I never will git to come home
again  I want you to tell all of my littel children houdy for me and kiss them
for me and tell them that I want to see them the worst that I ever did  I
hope that the Lord will spare my life to git home and see them once more
in this life Albert hufstutler [Huffstedler?] got shot through his neck the
other day  the last time I heard from him he was still alive I rote to you
about John Wadkins got killed on the 16 Day of last month you Rote that
Sidney got wounded in his elbow  I am sory to hear that  you Rote that
Joathan Walker was in the gard house  you dident Rite what it was for and
you Rote that tha give Henry Dale a good beating  that was good and you
Rote that your Brother had to start Back  I am sory to hear of that tho I
hope that the lord will Bless him  you Rote that you sent me a box and you
Rote that you sent me as good as you could git at that time What you sent
me is as good as I wanted I Did not think of making you mad Dear Wife  I
would not put any thing to trouble you if I can help it  I just thot that
Mother was abler to send me a box than you was and I Did not think any
harm  I Rote to her to not let my children suffer that is the last sent of
money that I have you Rote like that I tride to blitel [belittle] you I never
thought of any thing  you Rote that she never giv them any hing I dont
want you to think hard of me for it Dear Wife  I now that you love me and
I now that god nows that I love you and I will as long as I live  you Rote
that it had bin along time sence you seen me and it would not surprise me if
it dident be longer than it has bin before you see me yet tho I hope it wont
bee long you Rote that you was all ways one that wasant thought  you Rote
that god was your helper  he is all of our helpers if we put our trust in him
you Rote that you had not got no letter sence the 31 days of oct I have
Rote one are too ever week  I Dont now what is the Reason that you dont
git them I send this letter by James Duncon I hope that you will git it  I
have Rote for you to send me Sumthing more to eat of you could I wanted
you to send me sum beens & cabetch and one posum & apeace of pork  I
dont want you to send me much pork just alittel peace if you can cend me
any thing  you now what to send as well as I can tell you I Dont want you
to think hard of me  I want you to keep your lamp trimed and burning and

tell Thomas and Elizabeth to keep ther lamps trimed and burning  you can tell them that I still pray For them and I expect too as long as I live  I Dremp last night that I saw you and I Dremp that I got wounded in the hip and in the sholder  I hope and pray to god that I never will git wounded as long as I live  I send George Pinkney this Bill of money  you can tell him that his paw sent it to him

F.M. Poteet to M.A.E. Poteet

Farewell Dear wife for this time
I want to kiss you very bad

### Francis M. Poteet to Martha H. Poteet[19]

Peters Burg V.A.
December 31 1864

Dear wife and children

I Seat my Self this morning to write you a few lines to let you now that I am
well hoping that these lines may Reach your kind hands & find you all well
I hope and trust to the Lord that I may live to see you all again  it seems like
that will bee along time yet if I live I hope it wont  I have a grate desire to
see you all Once more in this life  I think that I could stay with you the
balans of my Days  I haint Received no letter from you in all most three
weeks  I would like to hear from you if I cant git to see you  I want you to
still pray for me and all the balans of the soldiers and tell all of my friends
to pray for me and to pray to god to spare my life to live to git home to
raise my littel Children  I have agrait desire to see you all one more  I have
heard Sum of the Soldiers Say that the pople thot tha Saw hards times at
home but  that tha dident not now what hard times was thare  I dont now
how times is thare  times is as hard thare as ha are hear  I dont now how you
all stand thare  we only git five littel Crackers for one day Rations we dont
git no  meat now but about twist a week  if that aint hard times I dont now
what hard times is  the mud is shoes mouth deep hear now and it tis A
snowing now as hard as it can  Rip my Shoes very bad but I dont now how
long it will bee till I git apare  I want you to Rite me all the newse and I
want you to tell Mooney to come badly  and stay till the war ends are stay
till the crowd comes home  tha all Say that tha Hear say that tha are agoing
to give us adiner the 2 day of next year  I dont now  I cant [rite?]  tha [doo?]
keepe so mutch [fuss?] O lord look down on me and spare my life to live to
git home and have mursy on my famly and save them from all harm and
Spare there lives to live to Give  I want you to send me sumthing to eat by
Mooney are Camp I Sent all of the letters that I had but the too last ones
that you sent  dont forgit to pray for me

F. M. Poteet to M. A. E. Poteet

## Martha H. Poteet to Francis M. Poteet[20]

Feb 2 1865

Dear husband

I seat my self to write you a few lines to night to let you know that we are tolerable well and I do hope that this will Reach your kind hands and find you well you sed if you had a mess of pudding you would be glad I haint made non this winter I kept one hot till after Camp went back to make you some pudding and sausage but he don so mean that didend get to send you any thing I dont expect G W Mooney will come back he says that there is anough to come without him and I dont know when I will get to send your socks there is a strong talk of peace here I hear that they have got a white flag hoisted there on both sids I want to know what you think about it they shot some of the Deserters the other day they saw the blood but didend get the man the Jonson crowd dos bad they think the soldiers will get home in a short time and I hope they will I hav bin walking to day and I hav got the headache and I cant half write and I hav to go to morrow or next day again to try to get a horse to plow if I can we have had some of the coldest wether that ever has ben hear the baby can walk a little it never crawled a bit I wish you could see the little stumpy thing I am afraid it is too smart it aint nine Months old and it can say several words if you was to start home afoot you never would get home the Mc dowell Melisha [McDowell County Militia] is at home now and they are after run aways evry day it is the burk Melisha [Burke County Militia} after them but they dont ketch many the sesesh [Secession]men dos hate to own that we are whiped they wont talk about it if they can help it it dos me good to tell it to them but they hav to own it old vance says that if they dont Make peace and let the men come home in time to make a crop that starvation will be at evry mans door and if they dont come it will be so I hate for you to suffer for the big men if you can come with a Company and keep out of the way I dont think thy will pester them bad if they dont do like the Johnson Crowd the children sends you howdy and I would be very glad to see you but I dont know whether I will ever see you any moor in this world but I hope I will see you soon the next day I am cleaning out the flax to day the first that I ever tride to clean and I dont think that I will try to clean any moor soon it has very nigh wore me out my back hurts so that I cant set still I sholy think that I hav as hard a time as any woman in the County if I have to do another year as I have this I think it will Finish me but I hope that you will get to come home to help me oh God spar the Life of My Dear husband to get home to his helpless family shield him from all harm and danger give him somthing to eat and ware and grant him a speedy return home oh Merciful God guard and protect my husband in all his trials and troubles and bring him safe through  this letter is wrote so bad I dont expect you can read it but if you can write me all the news  I must close by saying I remain your true loving Wife untill death  write soon

M. P. to F. P. May the Lord bless and save you farwell Francis

## McDowell County Collections

1. Catherine Carson letter to Gov. Zebulon B. Vance, 8 Jul 1864. The Zebulon Baird Vance Papers, vol. 15.5, p. 551, State Archives of North Carolina, Raleigh, North Carolina.

2. Francis M. Poteet letter to Martha H. Poteet, 12 Nov 1863. Poteet-Dickson Letters, 1861-1902. Hunter Library Digital Collections, Western Carolina University, Cullowhee, NC.

3. Francis M. Poteet letter to Martha H. Poteet, 23 Nov 1863. Poteet-Dickson Letters, 1861-1902. Hunter Library Digital Collections, Western Carolina University, Cullowhee, NC.

4. Martha H. Poteet letter to Francis M. Poteet, 7 Jan 1864. Poteet-Dickson Letters, 1861-1902. Hunter Library Digital Collections, Western Carolina University, Cullowhee, NC.

5. Martha H. Poteet letter to Francis M. Poteet, 21 Jan 1864. Poteet-Dickson Letters, 1861-1902. Hunter Library Digital Collections, Western Carolina University, Cullowhee, NC.

6. Martha H. Poteet letter to Francis M. Poteet, 4 Feb 1864. Poteet-Dickson Letters, 1861-1902. Hunter Library Digital Collections, Western Carolina University, Cullowhee, NC.

7. Francis M. Poteet letter to Martha H. Poteet, 8 Feb 1864. Poteet-Dickson Letters, 1861-1902. Hunter Library Digital Collections, Western Carolina University, Cullowhee, NC.

8. Martha H. Poteet letter to Francis M. Poteet, 18 Feb 1864. Poteet-Dickson Letters, 1861-1902. Hunter Library Digital Collections, Western Carolina University, Cullowhee, NC.

9. Francis M. Poteet letter to Martha H. Poteet, 23 Feb 1864. Poteet-Dickson Letters, 1861-1902. Hunter Library Digital Collections, Western Carolina University, Cullowhee, NC.

10. Martha H. Poteet letter to Francis M. Poteet, 7 Apr 1864. Poteet-Dickson Letters, 1861-1902. Hunter Library Digital Collections, Western Carolina University, Cullowhee, NC.

11. Francis M. Poteet and Thomas M. Hendley letter to Martha H. Poteet, 4 May 1864. Poteet-Dickson Letters, 1861-1902. Hunter Library Digital Collections, Western Carolina University, Cullowhee, NC.

12. Francis M. Poteet letter to Martha H. Poteet, 31 May 1864. Poteet-Dickson Letters, 1861-1902. Hunter Library Digital Collections, Western Carolina University, Cullowhee, NC.

13. Martha H. Poteet letter #1 to Francis M. Poteet, 16 Jun 1864. Poteet-Dickson Letters, 1861-1902. Hunter Library Digital Collections, Western Carolina University, Cullowhee, NC.

14. Martha H. Poteet letter #2 to Francis M. Poteet, 16 Jun 1864. Poteet-Dickson Letters, 1861-1902. Hunter Library Digital Collections, Western Carolina University, Cullowhee, NC.

15. Martha H. Poteet letter to Francis M. Poteet, 6-7 Oct 1864. Poteet-Dickson Letters, 1861-1902. Hunter Library Digital Collections, Western Carolina University, Cullowhee, NC.

16. Francis M. Poteet letter to Martha H. Poteet, 23 Oct 1864. Poteet-Dickson Letters, 1861-1902. Hunter Library Digital Collections, Western Carolina University, Cullowhee, NC.

17. Martha H. Poteet letter to Francis M. Poteet, 2 Nov 1864. Poteet-Dickson Letters, 1861-1902. Hunter Library Digital Collections, Western Carolina University, Cullowhee, NC.

18. Francis M. Poteet letter to Martha H. Poteet, 3 Dec 1864. Poteet-Dickson Letters, 1861-1902. Hunter Library Digital Collections, Western Carolina University, Cullowhee, NC.

19. Francis M. Poteet letter to Martha H. Poteet, 31 Dec 1864. Poteet-Dickson Letters, 1861-1902. Hunter Library Digital Collections, Western Carolina University, Cullowhee, NC.

20. Martha H. Poteet letter to Francis M. Poteet, 2 Feb 1865. Poteet-Dickson Letters, 1861-1902. Hunter Library Digital Collections, Western Carolina University, Cullowhee, NC.

# 11. WILKES COUNTY COLLECTIONS

## Civil War Collection: State Archives of North Carolina

One of the many Civil War letters in the State Archives was written by James W. Parlier. Parlier (1830-1869) was the son of Jonathan and Rebecca Parlier of Wilkes County, North Carolina. He was a farmer from the Pore's Knob area of Wilkes County. Parlier enlisted on September 23, 1862 and served as a private in Co. I, 26th NC Infantry. He survived the war, but died in 1869 and is buried in the Parlier Family Cemetery in Wilkes County. He married Phoebe Cook, the daughter of Ephraim and Lavenia Marlow Cook who died in April 1917. The Parliers had two children.

## Proffit Fanily Letters, 1860-1865, 1882

William Morgan Proffit and Mary Walsh Proffit lived near Lewis Ford Post Office in Wilkes County, North Carolina. They had four sons: William H. Proffit, Alfred N. Proffit, Andrew J. Proffit and Calvin L. Proffit. Jesse Miller was a son-in law of the Profitts, married to William and Mary's daughter, Elizabeth. William served in Company B, 1st NC Regiment, Alfred and Andrew both served in Company D, 18th NC Regiment, and Calvin was in Company H, 13th NC Regiment.

The only Proffit son to survive the war was Alfred who fought many battles and was present at the surrender of General Lee at Appomattox, Virginia. Alfred received several wounds during the war, and family lore says that one day he sneezed up a piece of minie ball which had been lodged in his sinus cavity for some time. Reportedly, this artifact is still in the family's possession.

## James W. Parlier to N.B. Parlier[1]

Jan the 11 1865
Camp near Petersburg Va


Dear Brother

it is threw the kind hand of Provedence I am bless with the opportunity of
droping you a few lines to let you no that I am as well as comon Truly
hoping this note will find you all well and hearty  NB I want to see you all
very bad and I can inform you that I recived your very kind leter dated the
5 of [Dec?] which gave me much Satisfaction to hear from you all you must
Excuse me for not writing To you Sooner for I have bin at the hospitle
parte of the tim and had a ball cut out of my hand  it was lodged against the
bones in the back of my haind  it nearly made me twist my tale when the
doctors was cuting it out but it is nearly healed up   I can sorty rit that is all
that I do  I dont do any duty at all  I haint done any since I came back [?]
nor shut my hand  nor never Expect to again  I think this cussed ware will
end soon and in the way I have thought all the time  N B the time is heard
here and I want you to send be a nother [box?] Please help Phebe to fickes
me another and send it to me for I dont get only half Enough to eat  Rit
soon and oftne

Yours
J  W Parlier to NB Parlier
truly fare well

## Andrew Proffit to His Parents William and Mary Proffit[2]

Near Martins burg Va
Sept. the 22th 1862

Dear Father and mother

It is with great pleasure that I write you a few lines which will inform you that we are in the land of the living and enjoying reasonable position of health etc. I have indeed stood the trip well and have no sickness. I have stood it better than the other boys. We have been gone one month & 2 days & have been in the battle the 15h at Harpers Ferry where where we took about 1000 Prisoners in Maryland which was indeed a bloody battle. We did not get to fire there but was exposed to the fire of the enemy in an open field for about one half mile. Severil of our Reg were killed and Wouned. We lay all day next day behind a fense exposed to their sharp shooters & A.W. Dunkin was shot through the thigh. That night we crossed back to va. We formed in line of battle about one mile from them and made a generil charge, exposed the whole way to the heaviest bombing said to be by old soldiers that they ever saw but we routed them and drove them back across the river about 9 or 10 oclock. I suppose we lost a great many but the yankees lay on the field in heaps and piles. We got all their arms, knapsacks, and all they had with many prisoners as they crossed the river.

We give them fits and I shot as long as we could see blue coat. Exposed to the fire of 3 batteries the bombs burst round our head with terrific fury and showers of grape and canister fell mingled with limbs of trees thick around us, but he God of heaven protected us from their power which I hope he will ever do. We were much exhousted from the fatigues of the charge that we threw away our clothes & blankits only what we have on but that is all right. We will get more. A.N. [his brother Alfred Newton Profit] was slightly struck on the arm with a piece of shell or something. He dropped his gun. I asked him if he was hurt. He said not. He grabbed his and fought like a heroe while the sweat dropped fast from his brow. T.G. Walsh, A. Vannoy, John Ferguson, R.M. Blankinship, Vincent Hindrix & others were engaged and fought like veterans. Wm. C. Proffit was struck on the knee with a piece of a bomb and knocked down so he did not go through but was not hurt much. He is not very well now but A.N & W. C. Have not stood it as well as I have but have kept up and done good service and for bravery can not be excelled. We have not been drilled exceeding 4 hours but our officers give us much praise for fighting.

Well Pa as it is all right on the goose about the war, I will now ask you a few questions. I want you to write me all the news about our domestic consensus. Have you bought you any land if so where & what price? Are you done fodering? Have you sold my Mare or Jack and what price? Have you made any trades of importance & what are they? DO we have any free school and who is teaching? Where is H.M. Stokes & what is he doing. If you have heard from Jesse Mills & how he is & how J. Betties family is doing and how the church is getting along. Pleas answer these interrogations and give me the news about the connection and neighbors and if cousin fanny got well. Write if you have heard from harriston lately. he was broken down and not able to travel when his Reg left the Rhapadan and he was sent back to Gordonsville or Orange Ct. to rest. I saw some of his reg yesterday. I thought that William Walsh was gone home when I wrote before but he did not start then but I suppose he has or will go soon for he will not be retained in service. Tell H. Binghams connection that I see him almost every day. He is in our brigade & is doing well. Pa – I want you to keep Calvin at home if possible in an honorable way. I know he will stay if he will continue to teach school for he is not able for such service as is required.

I believe I have written about all I know. I am anxious to hear from you & to know what you are going to do about at home. I know not what plan to suggest if you could get that set of mules I would be much pleased, if not, I think you could do well on Gap Creek. If you get a good chance you must do the best you can. Sell any of my property and apply it to the most needful purpose. Write whether Capt Ball took my wagons or not and take it all in. Get some man to write a day for you and write everything that will be of interest to me. Tell all my friends to write often to me & I will write to them but my chance is bad. I have to send them to Gordonsville to be mailed which is about 150 or 200 miles. There fore if you do not get many letters from us you need not be uneasy. When you write direct this in writing thus they will follow me where I am "A.J. Proffit, 18th Reg. NC Troops, Branch's Brigade, A.P. Hill's division, Gordonsville va. Co. D." I will now close close by subscribing my self you most obedient son till death, &c.

A.J. Proffit

PS – Please inform my friends how to direct their letters, &c. A.J.P.

## W. H. Proffit to His Father and Mother[3]

May 8th 1863

Dear father and mother:

I avail myself of this opportunity of informing you that I am still alive and in good health, although I have just passed through another of the bloodiest battles of the war. We have had another desperate battle on the Rappahannock, but I am glad to inform you that <u>victory is ours</u>. Our Regiment was in the hardest part of the battle and suffered severely. I received a wound in the jaw on Sunday evening and have since then been at the Hospital, but am not seriously injoured and will rejoin my company in a few days (The hospital to which I refer is near the battle field where the wounded were carried during the fight). I have not received any correct news from our connection & friends in other Regts. About 30 of our company are killed and wounded. Thomas Ellen, William Pilkenton, John Pennel, Samuel Pennel and J. N. Martin have all died on the field. John Estes had his right arm broken near his shoulder. Sergt. D. M. Carlton was slightly wound but is now at the company. Anderson Vannoy and, perhaps, others, of our co. who were your acquaintances are wounded.

I will write you again soon and give you fuller accounts. I will also very soon write Saml Walsh Jr.

Yours,

W. H. Proffit

## Andrew Proffit to His Father William Proffit[4]

Camp Lee Richmond va
May the 15th 1863

Mr. Wm. Proffit

Dear Father,

I take this kind opportunity of writing you a few lines which will inform you that I am again on the southern Soil, well and doing finely. I am sorry to inform you that I unfortunately fell into the hands of the enemy on Sunday the 3rd inst. I will now try to tell you how it happened as we were on the march to the battlefield. I with another corporal were appointed to guard the flag one of the most dangerous positions in battle on Saturday night there fell a bomb in my company & exploded in 4 or 5 feet of me & wounded the flag bearer and five or six of my Co. taking off one man's leg & wouded my lieutenant when the flag of my country fell to the earth I grabed it with my own hands my Colonel told me to thrown down my gun and hold on to my flag which I did that night the yankees charged on us but we soon repulsed them. next morning we made a charge on them routed them from their first breast works & proceeded to the second was ordered to charge them which part of us did I carried the flag to the breastworks we routed a long line of them & held our position but the 28th N.C. Regt on our right failed to charge them the enemy commenced fireing up our lines and give them a chance to retake their works again which give us no chance to escape I lay there with two lines of battle cross fireing at me at a short distance & three batteries throwing grape at me not more than 3 or 4 hundred yards distant the first I knew the yanks were in five steps when two jumped over the breast works & grabed the flag out of my hand & said to me fall in John ha. ha. ha. John fell in but did not like to do it

They took us to washington and kept us about 13 days they treated us with great respect give us plenty to eat when they brought us from Washington we came down the Potomac through Chesipeak bay by fortress Monroe then up the James river to Citty point near Petersburg where we landed. we came here to camp lee Richmond last night I do not know when we will be carried to our regiments but I suppose shortly I am unable to say what became of A.N. & W.H. A.N. give out the night before I was taken we had had nothing to eat for a day or so & marched hard which made him sick & he was sent back to the rear I think that nothing but fatigue & hunger was the matter W.H. was in the fight some of his Co. is here as prisoners they say that he was not hurt the last they saw of him & I hope he was not. My Col. was killed & my Lieut Col. was wouded. & the great Gen. Jackson was mortally wouded by his own men & is now dead.

father I am getting use to all kinds of hard ships in warfare & though I say it my self I know nothing of cowardice & God forbid that I ever should the lord has been very mercyful to me & I fear I have not a heart to praise him as I ought I want you & all my friends to remember me at a throne of grace I will now close give my warmest love to mother, [Sis?] and all my friends Write soon & direct to Co. D, 18th Regt N.C.T. Richmond Va.

I remain yours with great respect.

A.J. Proffit

## Jesse Miller to His Parents William and Mary Proffit[5]

Camp of the 53 Reg.
8 miles North East of Orange CH, Va
January 3rd 1864

Mr Wm and Mary Proffit

Dear Father and Mother I with grate pleasure drop you a short note which will in form you that I am in tolerable helth owing to hardships and privations of camp life. I do grately hoep when these lines come to hand you and famely may be Joying good helth.

I have no news for to communicate wich would inter rest you. I have no war news at presant times & all is still in this vicinity at presant & we have just got up some of our huts. I got mine done the first of this instant all to the done shelter. I had not laid in a house nor under a tent for eight months. We have just taken the wether as it came and you can give a guess how we have fard and the wether is powerful cold here at this time and we are scarce of blankets but if we can get to stay here in our huts I think we can do verry well.

We have a grate manny that is sick in our briggade and some ar dieing. John Wodey died at Orange the 15 of December. harrison Brown was sent off to the horse pittle yester Day. Barnet Owens was sent this morning. Boath was verry sick men. I have no thout that Owens will live . We have bin so exposed I feer that we shal have a grate Deal of sickness. Orders came round last nite to furlow one man for evry twenty men in camp that some of them will be coming home constantly.

We have a close time here at this time. Tha have cut our rashions down to a quarter of a pound of bacon and one pound of flower and every thirde day we dont get that. We drew to day one spoonful of shooger and not so much coffee and no bacon. We have close living.

I have bin looking for a letter from you for some time. I wrote you a letter just as soon as I herd W.H. Was ded but has failed to receave an answer yet & when these lines you receave please respond to me. So I will close by acknowledging my self as ever,

Jesse Miller     P.S. Write soon & often

## **Alfred N. Proffit to His Sister and Cousin**[6]

Petersburg v.a.
September 1 1864

R.L. Proffit & S.R. Walsh

Esteemeed sister and cousin yours of the 22nd is at hand and it did not fail to interest me vary mutch to learn that you war all well. I am glad to hear from those fine revivals in Wilkes & also your fine crops – wheat, turnips, corn etc. I should love to be thare to help you eat some vegitables as they are so dear here. I can hardly buy them.

I will give you the prices of a few artickels: Appls from 2 to 5 dollars per dozen. Peaches and the same for onions $3 per quart. Water mellons from 3 to 10 dollars a peace. Butter $15 per labs. Small loves of bread $2 a cake. Milck $4 per quart and other things according. I am glad to hear of your good prospect for potatoes for I just paid one dollar for four little things. I give you some account of our fight on the 20th inst so I will no more about it.

We are now in our breast works two miles south west of Petersburg. Thare are no yankees in our front nearer than one mile and a half but the picket duty is hard as our brigade is vary small. We are drawing vary good rations. We all have as mutch bread and meat as we want. Old strong bacon but we got some beef today.

Sarah inform me in your next of Unkle Andrew and Ant Mary and all the family of the brig and what Regts do thay belong, the health of cousin Piley's health etc. In form me how you like to live in Wilkes & what the prospect for Marages is. Write me soon and excuse me for my imposition by asking so many questions. I hope you will excuse me for not recollecting your name when you first wrote to me. Tell davy I should be proud to see her for I could tell her some rich jokes. We have lots of fun along the lines.

Sis and Sarah give my love and best wishes to all of my friends and consider your selves two of them. I am vary glad that you formed the resolution to give me a letter onse a week for I have looked in vain many a long day. Dont break your intention. Sis I send Julyan Miller a [illegible]. Tell the rest I have run out but if I have the chance I would make them all one. Give her it as soon as you can if ti is two small tell her to give it to one of the rest and I will make her another. These lines leaves me in the best of health hopeing that may find you same.

Yours as ever,
A.N. Proffit

**Andrew N. Proffit**

Wilkes County Collections

1. James Parlier letter to Noah Parlier, 11 Jan 1865. NC Digital Collections. State Archives of North Carolina: Civil War Collection.

2. Andrew Profitt letter to William and Mary Proffit, 22 Sep 1862. Proffit Family Letters, #3408-z. Southern Historical Collection, Louis Round Wilson Library, University of North Carolina at Chapel Hill.

3. W.H. Proffit letter to his Father and Mother, 8 May 1863. Folder 3, Proffit Family Papers. Southern Historical Collection, Louis Round Wilson Library, University of North Carolina at Chapel Hill.

4. Andrew J. Proffit letter to William Proffit, 15 May 1863. Folder 3, Proffit Family Papers, #3408. Southern Historical Collection. Louis Round Wilson Library, University of North Carolina at Chapel Hill.

5. Jesse Miller letter to William and Mary Proffit, 3 Jan 1864. Folder 4, Proffit Family Papers. Southern Historical Collection, Louis Round Wilson Library, University of North Carolina at Chapel Hill.

6. Alfred N. Proffit letter to his Sister and Cousin, 1 Sep 1864. Folder 4, Proffit Family Papers. Southern Historical Collection, Louis Round Wilson Library, University of North Carolina at Chapel Hill.

# References

Allen, W.C. The Annals of Haywood County, North Carolina. Literary Licensing, LLC. Whitefish, MT, 1935.

Avery Family of North Carolina Papers, 1777-1890, 1906 (collection no. 033). The Southern Historical Collection. Louis Round Wilson Special Collections Library. University of North Carolina at Chapel Hill.

Barrett, John G. "Governor Zebulon Vance." Dictionary of North Carolina Biography, 1979-1996. University of North Carolina Press. Web (accessed May 30, 2015).

Bynum, Victoria E. "Documents on the Shelton Laurel Massacre from the North Carolina State Archives." *Renegade South* (blog). April 13, 2009. http://renegadesouth.wordpress.com/2009/04/13/documents-on-the-shelton-laurel-massacre-from-the-north-carolina-state-archives/ (accessed May 21, 2015).

Chiliab Smith Howe Papers, 1814-1899. (collection 03092). The Southern Historical Collection. Louis Round Wilson Special Collections Library. University of North Carolina at Chapel Hill.

Daniel W. Revis Letters, 1862-1863. State Archives of North Carolina. North Carolina Digital Collections: Civil War.

Edmonston and Kelly Families Collection. Hunter Library Digital Collections, Western Carolina University, Cullowhee, NC.

Edmund Walter Jones Papers, 1789-1917 (collection no. 03543). The Southern Historical Collection. Louis Round Wilson Special Collections Library. University of North Carolina at Chapel Hill.

Edward W. Phifer, "Saga of a Burke County Family," The North Carolina Historical Review 39 (Winter, Spring, and Summer 1962) and William S. Powell, ed., Dictionary of North Carolina Biography, Vol. I, 1979.

Eliza Murphy Walton Letters, 1834; 1861-1863 (collection no. 02686-z). The Southern Historical Collection. Louis Round Wilson Special Collections Library. University of North Carolina at Chapel Hill.

Federal Census of 1860, Jackson County, North Carolina.

Inscoe, John C. and Gordon B. McKinney. The Heart of Confederate Appalachia: Western North Carolina in the Civil War. Chapel Hill: University of North Carolina Press, 2001.

James Watson Collection. Hunter Library Digital Collections. Western Carolina University, Cullowhee, NC.

Kimberly, Pruett. "150th Anniversary Renews Interest in Civil War letters at WCU." *The Macon County News,* 4 Aug 2011. Print.

Lenoir Family Papers, 1763-1940, 1969-1975. (collection no. 00426). The Southern Historical Collection. Louis Round Wilson Special Collections Library. University of North Carolina at Chapel Hill.

Major Wiley Parris Civil War Letters. Hunter Library Digital Collections, Western Carolina University, Cullowhee, NC.

McCoy, George W. "Confederate Armory Here Turned Out Superior Weapons." *Asheville Citizen-Times,* 13 Jan 1952. Print.

Moore, John W. 25th North Carolina Infantry Soldier Roster. Vol. 2.( 1882). http://www.civilwarindex.com/armync/soldiers/25th_nc_infantry_soldiers.pdf

Moore, John W. 9th North Carolina Regiment / 1st North Carolina Cavalry Soldier Roster. Vol. 1, (1882). http://www.civilwarindex.com/armync/soldiers/9th_nc_cavalry_soldiers.pdf

Osment, Timothy N. *The Shelton Laurel Massacre.* 2008. http://digitalheritage.org/2010/08/the-shelton-laurel-massacre/

Poteet-Dickson Letters, 1861-1902. State Archives of North Carolina. North Carolina Digital Collections: Civil War.

Proffit Family Letters, 1860-1865, 1882. (collection no. 03408-z). The Southern Historical Collection. Louis Round Wilson Special Collections Library. University of North Carolina at Chapel Hill.

Rugg, George. "The Shipman Family Correspondence." Rare Books and Special Collections: Manuscripts of the American Civil War, Hesburgh Library, University of Notre Dame, Indiana.

"Samuel Price Carson." *Historic Carson House.* 2008. Web.

"Shelton Laurel Massacre." NorthCarolinahistory.org. Web (accessed April 23, 2015).
http://www.northcarolinahistory.org/encyclopedia/660/entry/

Thomas George Walton Papers, 1779-1897 (collection no. 00748). The Southern Historical Collection. Louis Round Wilson Special Collections Library. University of North Carolina at Chapel Hill.

Walter Clark, ed., *Histories of the Several Regiments and Battalions from North Carolina in the Great War 1861-65.* Vols. 1 and 2. (1901).

Zebulon Baird Vance Papers (1824-1915)., North Carolina State Archives, Raleigh, NC.

Zebulon Baird Vance-Harriette N. Espy Vance Letters, 1851-1878. State Archives of North Carolina, Raleigh, NC.

Photo Credits

*Andrew N. Proffit.* http://civilwartalk.com/threads/the-proffit-brothers-of-wilkes-county-north-carolina.84797/. Web (accessed 2 Jun 2015).

*Augustus S. Merrimon.* 1875. North Carolina Museum of History. Raleigh, NC.

*Carson House.* N.d. Prints and Photographs Division, Library of Congress.

*Colonel Isaac E. Avery.* http://www.scvocr.com/camp-836-history.html. Web (accessed 1 May 2015).

*Colonel William H. Thomas.* http://www.nccivilwar150.com/history/war-within.htm. Web (accessed 15 May 2015).

*Dixie Hall.*
https://www.flickr.com/photos/ncccha/8544035055/in/photostream/. Web (accessed 27 Apr 2015).

*General Henry Heth.* N.d. Civil War Photographic Collection, Library of

Congress.

*Governor Zebulon Vance.* http://www.ourstate.com/zebulon-vance/. Web (accessed 1 Apr 2015).

*James A. Seddon,* Secretary of War. Pictures of the Civil War, Select Audiovisual Records, National Archives and Records Administration. Dickinson College. Carlisle, PA.

Johnston, Frances Benjamin. *Swan Ponds.* 1938. Library of Congress.

*Reward Poster.* 1869. Governors' Papers, William Holden, North Carolina Division of Archives and History.

Shuler, Laura S. *Creekside.* 2009. Private collection.

Tart, Edith W. *Zebulon Vance Birthplace.* 1936. North Carolina Museum of History. Raleigh, NC.

*Thomas George Walton.* Private collection, Walton Family. Morganton, NC.

*William Lenoir.* 1910-1930. North Carolina Museum of History. Raleigh, NC.

*William W. Avery.* N.d. NC Collection Photographic Archives. University of North Carolina at Chapel Hill.

*Zebulon Vance.* http://www.thevancehouse.org/Zebulon-B--Vance.html. Web (accessed 10 May 2015).

www.ingramcontent.com/pod-product-compliance
Lightning Source LLC
LaVergne TN
LVHW051507080426
835509LV00017B/1958